# Medical and Psychiatric Issues for Counsellors

# Medical and Psychiatric Issues for Counsellors

Brian Daines, Linda Gask
and Tim Usherwood

SAGE Publications
London • Thousand Oaks • New Delhi

SAGE Publications Ltd
6 Bonhill Street
London EC2A 4PU

SAGE Publications Inc.
2455 Teller Road
Thousand Oaks, California 91320

SAGE Publications India Pvt Ltd
32, M-Block Market
Greater Kailash – I
New Delhi 110 048

**British Library Cataloguing in Publication data**

A catalogue record for this book is available
from the British Library.

ISBN 0 8039 7506 6
ISBN 0 8039 7507 4 (pbk)

**Library of Congress catalog record available**

Typeset by Mayhew Typesetting, Rhayader, Powys
Printed in Great Britain by Hartnolls Ltd, Bodmin, Cornwall

For Joan, John and Vicki

# Contents

| | | |
|---|---|---:|
| *Acknowledgements* | | viii |
| *Preface* | | ix |
| 1 | Issues in Referral and Assessment | 1 |
| 2 | Issues in Ongoing Counselling and Supervision | 18 |
| 3 | Medical Conditions and their Treatment in Relation to Counselling | 37 |
| 4 | Psychiatric Conditions and their Treatment in Relation to Counselling | 65 |
| 5 | Ethical and Legal Issues | 107 |
| Appendices | | |
| 1 | Suggested Reading | 118 |
| 2 | Glossary | 119 |
| 3 | Counselling in Specific Medical and Psychological Conditions | 122 |
| 4 | Useful Organisations | 128 |
| 5 | Internet Addresses | 129 |
| 6 | Preparation for Termination of Practice | 130 |
| 7 | The Mental Health Act (1983) | 132 |
| 8 | A Classification of Personality Disorder | 134 |
| 9 | Dealing with Medical Emergencies | 136 |
| References | | 143 |
| Index | | 151 |

# *Acknowledgements*

There are many to whom we owe thanks for help in the writing of this book. In particular we would like to thank Colin Feltham for his valuable advice and constructive comments on early versions of the text, Tim Bond and Peter Jenkins for their help with the chapter on ethics, Frank Sullivan for reviewing the chapter on medical conditions, Angie Perrett for her advice about counselling in general practice, and the late Viv Ball for her original enthusiasm and inspiration.

# Preface

## Historical Tensions

At least since the time of Freud there has been controversy over whether those who are not medically qualified should engage in psychological forms of treatment. This is despite Freud's strong arguments supporting the case for 'lay analysis' (Freud, 1962). There has existed within the medical community a strong voice which has warned of the dangers associated with practitioners who are not properly trained to evaluate psychiatric and medical symptoms. On the other hand, there has never been a situation where the medical profession has had the trained practitioners or the resources to address more than a minority of the situations that might benefit from psychotherapy or counselling. As such it was more or less inevitable that this need would be filled by the growth of various forms of psychological help away from the supervision of doctors and psychiatrists. There has also been a certain sense of inevitability about the uneasy relationship that has existed between non-medical practitioners and the medical profession.

In this context it is easy to put most of the blame on the medical profession. There are, however, genuine difficulties in practising counselling outside of a medical setting. Also counsellors and others have sometimes overstated the extent to which psychological help can be expected to be effective in relation to certain conditions. Although some within medicine have tended to dismiss all counselling as at best irrelevant and at worst dangerous, some counsellors and alternative practitioners have dismissed much of medical work as ill-founded. As a consequence they have on occasions overstated greatly the role of psychological factors in the generation of physical illness.

## Recent Developments

Over the last 10 years or so a number of things have happened which have made the relationship between doctors and counsellors less polarised. There has been a recognition of the problems attached to the use of medication, especially tranquillisers, in the long-term treatment of psychological disorders. This has led to doctors considering other options and to many patients being resistant (sometimes unreasonably so) to medication and asking for counselling instead.

In addition, the role of psychological factors as predisposing and maintaining factors in physical illness is now better understood and more widely accepted. This has led to an interest in providing a package of treatment with both physical and psychological components, particularly for those suffering from illnesses having major roots in both areas (Davis and Fallowfield, 1991). The response of some counsellors to the softening stance of the medical profession has been to recognise more clearly the value of doctors' expertise and to come to value a co-operative approach where possible. Many counsellors working outside medical settings have sought to establish consultancy on psychiatric and medical issues as part of putting their practice on a professional footing.

This does not mean, though, that harmony reigns and that there are not many points of contention between practitioners in both areas. Some doctors still take the approach that patients who do not need psychiatric treatment should not be seeking counselling help, and will actively discourage their patients from doing so. Correspondingly, some counsellors deny the reality of mental illness and see all psychiatric treatments as misguided and oppressive.

## A Working Framework

It is not the place of this book to explore fully these philosophical and underlying issues which have filled many books larger than this! Although some of these points will enter into our discussion of particular situations, we have to set out with some broad assumptions which are best stated at the outset. One of the assumptions we will work within is the validity of psychiatry in the treatment of certain disorders which may come the counsellor's way. There are conditions which present mainly with psychological symptoms where counselling does not have a major contribution to make, and within this a smaller group where it may be harmful. Clients may need medication and hospitalisation and, in some cases, where the person's life or the life of others is at risk, these may need to be compulsory.

In relation to physical illness we shall accept that in most instances the causes are mainly physical or environmental and that the role of counselling is a peripheral one, both in prevention and treatment, except in relation to a limited number of conditions. However, counselling can often have a role to play in a number of areas. It may assist in helping the person to come to terms with what has happened and in some instances help in pain control. There can also be benefits in helping to reduce stress, which can sometimes make relapse less likely and ongoing treatment more effective. The rationale for what follows is that the concerns of counselling and medicine, especially psychiatry, are closely related and that the counsellor needs to have a grounding of knowledge in these areas. This will not make the counsellor an expert, nor equipped to make either diagnoses or recommendations about treatment. The intention is more to alert the counsellor to situations where advice or referral should be sought. It is important that we are all aware of our limits to competence, as required in most counsellors' codes of ethics, and that we know what to do when we are faced with such situations.

The counsellor's approach will be very much influenced by a theoretical perspective. In the course of a short book it is not possible to deal with the issues from all the major theoretical perspectives, so a broad psychodynamic approach is taken with some occasional reference to other perspectives. This book may also reflect in parts a closer relationship between the activity of the counsellor and the client's GP than many counsellors practise. In the relationship between the client's counsellor and her GP, our view is that contact and co-operation are at least desirable and often essential for the well-being of clients, and we hope without being over-prescriptive to promote a re-think of ways of operating where this is appropriate.

This book is primarily directed to those who operate within a clear counselling framework, but we hope that others who use counselling as part of their work will also find it of value. Particular problems attach to combining counselling with other activities, such as advocacy, and it is beyond the scope of this book to explore these. Some of the boundary issues that arise, however, form part of the discussion of ethics in Chapter 5. Much confusion surrounds the similarities and differences between counselling and psychotherapy. These terms are used synonymously by some and in a clearly different way by others, although with no consistency in the differences. A substantial clarification of definitions has been carried forward by the Advice, Guidance, Counselling and Psychotherapy Lead Body, a government sponsored initiative. Organisations such as the British Association for Counselling and the UK Council for Psychotherapy have taken part in this process. One of the clearest differences between counselling and psychotherapy that this group has suggested is that counselling is a skills-orientated activity and psychotherapy is more based in theory, but practitioners from both fields encounter the kinds of issues raised in this book.

**Summary**

The first two chapters look at the way in which challenges to the counsellor's knowledge and skill may arise at various points in the counselling process, and aim to help the counsellor think through situations and, where necessary, make decisions and take action. The first looks both at those that arise at the point of referral and those that may arise during the process of assessment. It is important that the counsellor is able to have discussions with referrers, and clients making direct contact, about the appropriateness of the referral that take account of relevant medical and psychiatric information. In assessment it is often important to be able to elicit and evaluate the client's past and present medical and psychiatric history before making any decision about ongoing counselling.

The second chapter considers how to manage the situation where medical or psychiatric conditions emerge during the course of counselling, either because they occur part way through counselling, or because they have been hidden. There are also issues to address when illness or psychological disturbance occurs in the counsellor's own life. The final chapter deals with ethical issues which are becoming increasingly relevant as counselling seeks to establish itself further as a profession and clients become more aware of the standards they can expect from professionals and how to complain if they are not met. Situations relating to responsibility or care, limits to competence and confidentiality are particularly relevant.

Chapter 3 looks at medical conditions and their treatment in relation to counselling. Using the distinction between signs of illness that the counsellor can recognise, and the symptoms that clients may talk about, we then go on to discuss particular problems in physical health which the counsellor can learn to recognise, and what sort of response to these the counsellor should make. Additionally, both the impact of medical conditions and treatments on counselling and the potential positive and negative effects of counselling are considered.

Chapter 4 addresses psychiatric conditions and their treatment in relation to counselling. This is approached from the viewpoint of assessing the problems that the client presents, rather than from a starting point of diagnosis. Important aspects covered are helping the counsellor to recognise serious mental health problems and to understand the effects of drugs prescribed for psychiatric conditions.

The final chapter deals with the ethical and legal issues that can arise around medical and psychiatric issues in the work of a counsellor. An important part of this is trying to establish the boundaries to the counsellor's duty of care to clients in relation to their psychological and physical health. The ways in which this may vary according to the setting in which the client is seen are considered, and relevant sections of the BAC Code of Ethics and Practice for Counsellors are identified and discussed. Although we have tried to give sound advice based on current understandings in the various disciplines that impinge on counselling in this context, we cannot be responsible for the way in which this information and guidance is used by practitioners. We have stressed the importance of counsellors having multiple sources of support and advice, especially in dealing with difficult situations.

# 1

# *Issues in Referral and Assessment*

## Referrals

The issues surrounding the referral and assessment of clients are inherently complex and are made more so where medical and psychiatric factors are part of the situation. A basic decision that the counsellor has to make is whether counselling is appropriate to the person's circumstances and needs. Sometimes there is pressure to make a preliminary decision on the spot, such as when a GP who wants to make a referral asks for advice or a decision over the telephone. Whilst the ultimate decision about whether a person is offered a period of counselling has to be the outcome of a more thorough assessment, it can be disappointing for clients to be referred and then turned down as unsuitable for further sessions. Consequently, there is some pressure on counsellors not to see people for initial appointments unless there is a clear indication that such a session, either in itself or as a way of setting up further appointments, has value for the client. Some counsellors may prefer to work with clients and allow issues to emerge over a period of time from what clients choose to disclose rather than ask questions or undertake a formal process of assessment. Whereas counsellors may see their approach as deriving from their theoretical perspective (for example, client-centred or analytic), our view is that this is unwise and carries ethical risks (see Chapter 5).

On other occasions the counsellor may receive a referral letter, perhaps with very sketchy details about the potential client. These, though, may be enough to raise the counsellor's concerns about the possible psychiatric or medical complexities involved and whether the person can benefit from counselling. Where the counsellor and referrer work together on an ongoing basis a standard referral form giving basic information about the person, the reasons for the referral and the referrer's expectations from the counselling may be helpful.

## Additional Information about Referrals

Faced with such a situation, it may be wise to contact the referrer for more information before arranging to see the client. Often an explanation of why the referral has been made and how the referrer believes the person will benefit from counselling will be more useful than further details about the person's problems. The counsellor may also pick up in any discussion with the referrer what the client has been told to expect, and whether this might have been a help or a hindrance in facilitating a positive attitude to counselling. One of the dangers of going down the path of gaining more information about the person is that the situation can come to appear more complex rather than less, and the counsellor begins to take on board other people's opinions and prejudices which may cloud the assessment of the client if and when this eventually takes place. An additional hazard is that referrers are often in busy jobs and much time and energy may be consumed in chasing them or long delays may ensue if the matter is conducted by post.

## The Referrer's Agenda

One of the situations the counsellor needs to guard against is where clients are referred because the person at present helping them has not thought out clearly the reason for the referral, just does not know what to do with the person or, worse, thinks it is someone else's turn to put up with them for a bit! Some may be tempted to think that if the request is coming from a medical source (or another equally respected profession) then it must be a good idea. However, referrals from a medical source may be no more informed than those from other sources, and sometimes less. It is important for the counsellor to recognise fully and own her own area of expertise and professional judgement. Counsellors have a role in educating other professionals about the relevance of counselling and its limitations, and to encourage them to consider alternative options for referral, such as psychiatrists, community psychiatric nurses or social workers, where appropriate.

An important aspect in considering the referral may be whether a psychiatric or medical input will continue alongside that of the counsellor. This may offer considerable benefits, as the counsellor can proceed with the knowledge that someone is taking responsibility for particular areas of the client's care. The potential disadvantage can be that, in certain areas, there may be an overlap of responsibility and input that leads to confusion or the playing off of one professional against the other by the client. Successful multiple professional involvement needs clear boundaries, and good communication within a context of mutual trust between the professionals involved. These dilemmas will arise in slightly different ways for counsellors who work in medical settings (Higgs and Dammers, 1992: 34).

### Self-referrals

Some clients who self-refer will have already discussed this course of action with their doctor and enlisted their support in going ahead with exploring how counselling may be of benefit. However, this will not always be the case, and counsellors accepting self-referrals are regularly faced with clients who are involved with psychiatrists and other doctors. Often the attitude of these clinicians to counselling in general, and to the possibility of counselling for their patients in particular, is not known to the counsellor. Where the person is receiving psychiatric treatment or where there is a clear connection between a person's physical illness and the counselling they may receive, it is clearly desirable that any counselling is carried out with the support of the doctor involved.

However, it is generally reasonable at least to respond to an enquiry about counselling by arranging an initial assessment appointment without consulting any professionals who are already involved. For example, some counsellors work in settings where appointments are made for assessment without the opportunity for any discussion about the person's situation or reason for seeking counselling. However, it is not generally ethical for the counsellor to approach the person's doctor, either to gauge the

**Sample Information Sheet for Referrers**

Valley Counselling Agency
Crookes Valley Grove
Sheffield S10 1JJ
Tel: 0114-322-5091 (9 a.m. to 5 p.m. weekdays)

The Valley Counselling Agency is a community service established in the mid-1970s. We are widely used by the NHS, social services and other organisations and also accept self-referrals. We offer mainly short-term individual work along psychodynamic lines – generally, ten weekly sessions. The service operates to high professional standards and all our counsellors have obtained, or are working towards, accreditation with the British Association for Counselling.

We offer counselling for a wide variety of difficulties and can advise about the suitability of a possible referral if you would like to ring us. In practice we mainly see people experiencing difficulties with anxiety, depression or in their relationships, but we also commonly work with those experiencing eating disorders, the consequences of sexual abuse and other problems. The kind of counselling we offer looks at both people's present situation and their past history, and in particular explores the links between the two. We do not charge fees, but clients are invited to make a donation for each session.

Our aim is to offer an assessment appointment within ten working days and to offer regular appointments within two months of the assessment. Every effort is made to offer appointment times that are convenient, but waiting times may be longer if someone's availability is restricted. Where a formal referral is made, a short report is sent to the referrer following the assessment. It is also our policy, with clients' consent, to inform GPs when they begin and end their period of counselling with us.

The kind of counselling we offer usually requires that others are not involved in giving similar help. We do recognise, though, that there may be a need for complementary help – for example, in the form of medication. Where other professionals are involved, we, with clients' consent, liaise with them and try to foster a co-operative working relationship in the best interests of clients.

Before the assessment appointment clients are sent a pack of information about our agency, including clear directions about how to find us. At this first appointment the counsellor obtains as clear a picture as possible of the person's difficulties. Following this, an explanation of any counselling that is proposed is given, including any risks or alternatives. Clients are encouraged and helped at this interview to set their own aims and to ask questions about the agency and any help that is being offered or proposed.

John Wilmott
Senior Counsellor

appropriateness of counselling or the practitioner's attitude to it, without permission from the enquirer.

*Jean referred herself for counselling and attended for an assessment appointment during one of her periodic crises. During the course of this session it became clear that Jean had been under the care of psychiatrists in the past, and had probably been diagnosed as having a serious mental illness. This, together with other aspects of her problems that emerged during the session, led the counsellor to be unsure about whether counselling would be an appropriate response. Alongside discussing the matter with his supervisor, the counsellor, with the client's permission, contacted her GP to discuss the appropriateness of counselling. As a result of this it came to light that Jean had recently been seen by a psychiatrist who had felt that counselling would be helpful. This was valuable to the counsellor in coming to a decision to offer a series of appointments to her.*

## The Influence of Setting

Particular considerations may arise as a result of the setting in which the counsellor is working. Clients sometimes approach those working in private practice or charitable organisations out of a desire to avoid contact with the medical profession, and assume that no liaison with their GP will be needed. Similarly, counsellors working in the independent sector in complementary health clinics may particularly see clients who have a fear or mistrust of doctors or who may be unwisely avoiding consulting their doctor. On the other hand, counsellors in primary care may particularly see those who tend to turn to their doctor for help as a first preference.

*John came for an initial appointment after being persuaded by some friends to look for help. His main complaints were of social isolation and difficulties in making relationships, but in the course of the session he revealed that he believed that personal messages were being sent to him via his television. Exploration of this revealed a number of other delusional beliefs. The counsellor also discovered that he was not registered with a GP and was not open to the idea of doing so or of having any contact with the medical profession in relation to his problems. Despite the*

---

**Sample Liaison Letter to GP**

Dr H.K. Francis,
120, Watery Street,
Sheffield S3 4RN

Dear Dr Francis,

Re: Mr P.D. Atkinson d.o.b. 21.05.71
    35, Amberley Street, Sheffield S14 2ND

This man came to see me recently for counselling in relation to his feelings of depression and isolation. I understand that he has not been to see you about these difficulties and so I thought that, with his permission, I should write to you.

I feel we have identified some clear areas that he wishes to work on which are related to his current state of mind. I have agreed to see him initially for six sessions with the possibility of continuing for further sessions if appropriate. I hope that this arrangement is satisfactory as far as you are concerned, and will certainly recommend that he comes to see you should this prove necessary. If you do envisage any difficulties in my seeing him for counselling, I would be grateful if you could contact me.

Yours sincerely,

Jane Williams
Senior Counsellor

---

*potential pitfalls, the counsellor judged that John's interests were best served by offering him counselling. Important considerations in this were that at least he would have some form of therapeutic help and that it seemed unlikely that refusal would lead to his seeking more appropriate help. The counsellor felt able to take him on for counselling because she had access to medical advice and had had experience in counselling clients with psychotic illness.*

## Care Plans

Where a person is already having help from the mental health services an important question arises concerning the relationship of the counselling to the help which the client is already receiving. Ideally, there should be a care plan for the client, and it should be

---

**Sample Letter to Client Refusing Counselling**

Ms H. Thompson,
45, Howard Street,
Rotherham,
S. Yorks S65 4RR

Dear Ms. Thompson,

As promised, I am writing to you following our session on Wednesday to let you know my thoughts about your request for counselling. Your position is a quite complicated one and, as I said then, I needed more time to think about your situation and to ask advice from my colleague. My main concern is that at the moment you do not have the general support in your life to deal with the kinds of things that counselling might bring up.

As you have just moved from London you have not had the chance to make many friends and have not yet made contact with a GP here. I think that it would not be very helpful for you to go back from sessions here to spend most of your week in a flat on your own.

I do understand that you feel it is time to find something different from the psychiatric help you have been receiving over the last five years and do not want to close the door to your getting help from us. I suggest that you register with a GP and discuss your needs with him or her, and also give yourself time to become more established here. Then, if you would like to come to see us again in about six months' time, we could look again at taking you on for counselling.

Yours sincerely,

John Wilmott
Senior Counsellor

---

clear how the proposed counselling fits into this as part of an overall approach. Where the help a person is receiving is *ad hoc* or fragmented, then the counsellor may need to act as a catalyst in bringing about a case conference to ensure a coherent approach. Without this the client may be subject to confusion and to contradictory ideas from different carers. Fragmentation and conflict in the overall care that a client receives will be particularly problematic where they mirror the client's internal state. In cases of physical illness it is also desirable that there should be a coherent approach, particularly where there are strong psychosomatic elements to the client's illness.

## Rejecting Referrals

In order to justify not accepting a referral, a counsellor must be convinced that to see the person, even for assessment, would be totally inappropriate, or harmful. One situation where it might be inappropriate is where the enquirer makes it clear that his definition of confidentiality precludes any contact between the counsellor and those already involved in treating him. One factor that may also be influential is the work setting of the counsellor. Those working with comprehensive and accessible medical back-up will be able to consider referrals that those working in a more isolated setting may not. Counsellors also have to accept that, even with the best assessment, situations may remain unclear and uncertainties about what to do have to be tolerated and monitored as the counselling proceeds.

*Bill and Sue, a couple in their mid-twenties, came for help with their marital difficulties. In the course of assessment it was revealed that a paediatrician was seeing them with their daughter to deal with her problem of soiling. It was clear from their description of the appointment that she was beginning to suspect that their problems as a couple were connected with this, and consequently was beginning to work with them on relationship issues. The counsellor made it clear that some clear boundaries would need to be set up between this treatment and any proposed more intensive couple counselling and that this would involve the paediatrician knowing about the latter. Even after explanations and explorations of their resistance to the idea, the couple were unwilling that anyone should know about their coming to the counsellor and therefore no further sessions were possible.*

## Dilemmas Arising Particularly in Medical Settings

Those working in medical settings may face particular dilemmas. Sometimes these arise in the nature of the referral. For example, a person may have gone to see their GP for medication, but end up being referred to the practice counsellor instead, when that is not what they want. As a response they may try to enlist the support of the counsellor against the GP's assessment of what is appropriate. The counsellor may find herself in a dilemma where she agrees with the GP's idea about what is appropriate, but

**Table 1.1**  *Referral checklist – particularly for referrals from professionals*

1  Has the referrer a rationale for counselling for the client?
2  What has the client been told to expect from the counselling by the referrer?
3  Has the referrer a clear idea of what counselling may achieve?
4  Is the referral made on the basis that the goal of the counselling will be an improvement in a physical condition?
5  What has the client been told by the referrer about what to expect from counselling? Is what has been said likely to prove helpful or unhelpful?
6  Are any expectations of counselling unrealistic?
7  Are there other equally or more appropriate alternatives which the referrer might consider?
8  Are there any obvious indications against counselling?
9  Is further information needed before making a decision about moving on to a face-to-face assessment with the client?
10  Are other professionals already involved and, if so, is the referral part of a thought-out care plan?

**Table 1.2**  *Referral checklist – particularly for self-referrals*

1  Do those who may be involved in the person's treatment already know about/ support the possibility of counselling?
2  What reasons has the person for thinking counselling may help?
3  Is the goal of the counselling to be an improvement in a physical condition?
4  Is the person expecting counselling to cure an underlying psychiatric condition?
5  Do you observe or sense signs of underlying or hidden problems of a medical or psychiatric nature?
6  Are there physical or psychiatric conditions that may be precipitated by counselling? If so, is sufficient support available to deal with what might happen?
7  Have you access to the medical and psychiatric back-up needed to take this referral?
8  If help from others is already being offered, does counselling make sense as part of an overall care plan?

recognises that no treatment is going to be effective without the co-operation of the client. Another difficulty can be where the counsellor feels that the patient's physical symptoms are not being taken seriously. Hopefully, a situation will exist where such matters can be discussed constructively between the counsellor and the GP, but in situations where the GP feels that his judgement is being questioned, it may present a difficulty in staff relationships that is hard to resolve.

*Tom was referred to the GP counsellor for help with his depression. Exploration of the difficulty experienced by the counsellor in establishing a working relationship revealed that Tom had gone to his GP for anti-depressants. He did not want counselling, but in the face of the GP's decision had not seen any alternative to being compliant. The counsellor encouraged him to go back to the GP to discuss his treatment further. She also brought up at the next practice meeting the importance of referrals for counselling being made with patients' consent and understanding.*

## Assessment

In assessing a client for counselling it is important to try to elicit information about relevant psychiatric and medical conditions that are currently being treated. Knowing whether various illnesses have occurred in the past may also be valuable as part of assessment. With some, these details will be available at referral; with others, the client will reveal them without prompting. The counsellor needs, though, to be able to lead the client into discussing these areas without being too intrusive or adopting an interrogatory style. In this, having an idea of the kinds of questions and comments that might facilitate the process is helpful.

### Undiagnosed Psychiatric Conditions

It is more difficult to assess the possible existence of conditions that may as yet be undiagnosed. The counsellor cannot operate with the expertise of a psychiatrist or GP, but must be able to form a credible judgement about whether a recommendation or referral to see a medical practitioner is needed. Ultimately, the guideline must be that, if in doubt, the counsellor should seek advice or recommend that the client consults his or her GP. In general, the counsellor needs to be proactive in dealing with possible psychiatric features and to be aware of the possibility of physical symptoms. By this we mean that part of a counselling assessment is to identify the degree to which someone has depression, anxiety and panic states, obsessive and compulsive disorders and so on; and to discover any signs of major mental illness such as delusions. Again, the counsellor usually cannot

---

**Possible Assessment Questions – recognised conditions**

Have you ever discussed this with your doctor?
Have you had help with this in the past?
Are there any other people helping you at present?
Are you taking any tablets at the moment?
Do you have any problems with your health?
Have you ever had any serious illnesses or accidents?
Has your doctor ever suggested that you see someone else about this?

---

bring the necessary technical expertise to these areas. It is more that, by becoming experienced in knowing what is within his or her competence, the counsellor comes to recognise those areas that fall outside of it.

Having identified a particular problem – a moderate level of depression, for example – it is then often difficult to know what to do about it. At what point does depression cease to be something that can and should be contained within counselling? How much should the counsellor be influenced by the client's wishes and by the kind of approach the counsellor thinks will be used by the person's GP or local psychiatric services? There are no definitive answers to such questions, and in each individual case a decision often only emerges out of a careful consideration and balancing of interests and possible future scenarios. It is also important to remember that assessment is not just something that takes place at the point of referral, but that counsellors should be involved in an ongoing process of monitoring and assessment. Therefore, in some instances, it is valuable and appropriate to wait and see what emerges once the counselling is under way.

*Linda, a woman of 20, was referred for counselling by her GP as a result of fights that were developing between her and her boyfriend. Although there were various reasons for tension in the relationship, she described a preoccupation with violent fantasies and disturbing dreams in which violence and blood were predominant themes and she was the perpetrator. Careful questioning revealed these to be unusual, but with no indication that they were part of a psychotic illness. This also seemed to be the conclusion of the GP. A course of counselling was offered and she was put on the waiting list, although some ambivalence was expressed and some interest in obtaining a second opinion from a psychiatrist. By the time she reached the top of the waiting list Linda was in the care of a psychiatrist, her fantasies having become more clearly delusional in the meantime, and counselling did not proceed.*

## Undiagnosed Physical Conditions

Again in the area of physical illness the counsellor probably has no particular expertise, but with some knowledge and experience can begin to recognise the kinds of ways in which psychological problems manifest themselves and, by recognising those that cannot easily be accounted for within a psychological framework, comes to recognise some symptoms that may need investigation. This applies, for example, to some neurological conditions where the loss of concentration and memory is qualitatively different from that associated with, say, stress or depression. Striano (1988) discusses physical conditions which may present as psychological problems, and Cooper (1973) gives two case histories providing salutary lessons where physical illness was wrongly diagnosed as psychological disorder.

*Mary, a retired solicitor in her early sixties, was recommended to see a particular counsellor by a friend who had been helped by him. She complained of difficulties in her memory which, to the counsellor, did not seem to be the kind normally produced by anxiety, stress or depression. In addition, Mary did not seem to have any of these problems and he suggested that she consult her GP about a neurological referral. This led to a diagnosis of pre-senile dementia in its early stages.*

At the point of assessment, it is important to try to negotiate with the client an area of common understanding of what counselling might be able to offer. In particular, there is a need to avoid a situation where clients embark on counselling with a totally unrealistic idea of its curative possibilities in relation to their physical illness. This may be part of a denial of the illness and its consequences, and the counsellor would be wise to try to avoid collusion with this kind of denial. On the other hand, such mechanisms are there to a minor degree in most clients and may form part of what is worked with in the counselling, but without the gross idealisation of the counselling process. It has also to be acknowledged that, in many areas of physical illness, the value or otherwise of counselling is unclear. Therefore, in taking up a particular position in this area, we must be careful to recognise and give due weight to the situation where a client takes a different opinion from us. This is particularly so when the client's view would also be taken by some of our reputable colleagues.

The counsellor needs to keep up with current developments in the possible benefits of counselling to those with chronic illnesses. Interventions such as crisis counselling and work with families and in groups have been shown to reduce emotional distress in those suffering from chronic illness (Taylor and Aspinwall, 1990: 29). Counsellors using a behavioural approach need to be acquainted with the techniques which have been developed to help people with a wide range of conditions. For example, Pearce and Wardle's book (1989) includes contributions, amongst others, on hypertension, cardiac rehabilitation, head injury, chronic pain, diabetes and respiratory disease. Broome (1989) draws together contributions relating to the psychological understanding of a large number of illnesses, and a wide range of possible psychological approaches are covered in the discussion of the psychological treatment of these. Palmer and Dryden (1995), in their book on stress counselling, discuss health and lifestyle interventions in relation to alcohol intake, blood pressure, caffeine intake, smoking and weight control. A recent book by Pollin (1995) looks at working short-term with those having chronic illnesses. A summary of the literature on counselling approaches to various conditions forms Appendix 3.

## Conflicts of View

This brings us to the difficult problem of differences in opinion within and between professions. This was touched on above when we suggested that the particular kind of treatment for depression that a client might be offered by his GP or local mental health services might influence the outcome of the counsellor's assessment of a depressed client. Whereas the general direction has been towards increased tolerance between professions and viewpoints, we do need to recognise both that a proportion of medical practitioners have a negative view of counselling and that some counsellors have serious doubts about many standard ways of dealing with psychiatric disorders. In addition, counsellors may be aware that, whilst some of their clients may need medication or sanctuary, the setting in which these might be offered could preclude their obtaining the counselling that they need alongside this.

If the client is going to need psychiatric input as well as counselling, then obviously it is in the client's interests to try to set up some complementary forms of help and to avoid opposition and choice between the possibilities. In this it is helpful if the counsellor can try to develop good links and relationships with the relevant professionals in the community. It is important to recognise that the level of expertise and range of treatment options available from mental health services can vary greatly on a geographical basis, even within a city. Most practitioners will respond well to an approach from a counsellor who deals with matters in a professional manner and seeks to foster a co-operative working environment. They do not respond well to counsellors who try to tell them what to do, who reveal a hostile attitude to the ways in which they work with their patients or subject them to 'labelling'!

In making a referral or liaising with other professionals it is important to obtain the client's consent and not to behave in ways that are going to undermine their trust. This includes keeping them informed of the steps that you have taken and discussing with them at each stage the reasons for your actions and the possible outcomes. Some counsellors consider it good practice to show their clients what they have written about them in such cases of referral or liaison, or to provide them with copies of the letters sent. For the counsellor working within a general practice or psychiatric setting these concerns are often more easily dealt with, as the understanding of the setting will be that there is contact and liaison between various members of the team. There may be a different problem, however, in that the counsellor may not be able to establish a strong enough boundary around the counselling where other team members may feel entitled to know what is going on in the counselling and to act upon such information as they see fit.

The counsellor needs to be aware that some other professionals will have serious doubts about the effectiveness of counselling, or of a particular form of counselling, and may have concerns that it

---

**Sample Letter to GP**

Dr F.D. Mason,
The Vale Medical Centre,
Spring Vale Walk,
Sheffield S6 4RJ

March 20th, 1996

Dear Dr Mason,

Re: Mr M.J. Fitzpatrick d.o.b. 03/06/70
24, Roebuck Avenue, Sheffield 6

I am writing to you about this man whom I believe is one of your patients. He came to me recently asking for counselling help with his anxiety, for which he says he received medication from you a few months ago. With his permission I am contacting you on two counts; firstly to check out that you have no objections to my seeing him for ten weekly sessions of counselling, and secondly to share my concerns about some physical symptoms which he described to me.

He reports that for the last two weeks he has been suffering from headaches and dizzy spells. I realise that these may be related to the stress he is undergoing at work which is leading him to experience high levels of anxiety. However, I have suggested that he comes to see you about these new symptoms and also wanted to let you know directly about my concerns.

Yours sincerely,

John Wilmott
Senior Counsellor

---

could actually do harm (Eysenck, 1992). These concerns may apply to either physical or psychological states and may in certain instances be well founded. Particularly with psychotic states and serious physical illness there may not be benefit to be gained from working with a person in a way that undermines their psychological defences and increases their awareness of their underlying psychological state (see also Chapter 3).

*Craig came for an assessment appointment asking for help with fears about losing control of himself, which seemed to the counsellor to be delusional. Taking a history from him revealed that he had been under the psychiatric services for many years, was on medication and was still seeing a psychiatrist for occasional appointments. A picture also emerged of someone who was socially isolated and found it hard to cope with relationships. The counsellor felt that it was necessary to discuss the situation with his GP and obtained Craig's permission to do this. The GP advised against an approach that would explore and concentrate his attention on the delusional ideas, but was supportive of a short period of counselling focused on his social difficulties. The counsellor decided to accept this advice and offered Craig six sessions to work on this area, which he accepted and from which he benefited.*

### Referring On

One outcome of the assessment session may be that the client needs to be referred on, and it can be difficult to achieve this without the client feeling rejected or demoralised. It is important to recognise the client's feelings in this. Initially, there may be disappointment at not being able to see the counsellor again. This may be offset by a recognition of what has been achieved in the one session. People understandably tire of having to repeat their story to a number of professionals before they are able to find the right place to obtain help. It is important for the counsellor to recognise any shortcomings in the referral system, but also to keep in mind that it is inevitable that a proportion of clients will not end up in the right place at the first attempt, especially with multi-faceted problems involving medical or psychiatric as well as psychological and emotional dimensions.

### The Role of Supervision

In all these areas the counsellors can be considerably aided by their supervisors, who can help the supervisee to establish a number of points. These include:

- whether the person will benefit from counselling;
- whether the counselling needed is within the counsellor's competence;
- pointing to evidence in clients of medical/psychiatric problems;

- clarifying the nature of any medical/psychiatric problems;
- avoiding setting up unrealistic aims in the counselling;
- appropriate liaison with medical and mental health professionals; and
- the resolution of ethical dilemmas.

In turn, supervisors need to ensure that they have the appropriate training and experience to lead supervisees through these areas of their work. Some other general issues to do with supervision of these aspects of counselling work are dealt with at the end of the next chapter.

## Conclusion

A sound system of dealing with referrals and a professional standard of assessment underlies good practice in counselling. This is as true for these areas of medical and psychiatric matters as for others. The following are important parts of such good practice:

- an adequate system for screening referrals;
- an assessment procedure that maximises the possibility of detecting existing medical and psychiatric conditions and current treatments for them;
- an approach to clients that is caring, respects their autonomy and right to confidentiality, involves them in decision-making and seeks their best interest;
- an approach to medical practitioners and other staff that is professional, businesslike and respectful and seeks co-operative solutions in the best interests of clients;
- working with an awareness of the other relevant ethical issues in this area, including working within limits to competence.

# 2

# *Issues in Ongoing Counselling and Supervision*

## Hidden Issues

There are two main ways in which medical or psychiatric issues may arise during the course of ongoing counselling. In some instances it will be because these were hidden at the beginning of counselling. They may have been hidden from the counsellor by the client, or the client may have been unaware of them or their relevance. Alternatively, such problems may occur part way through counselling, often as unwelcome intrusions that disrupt both the process and progress of counselling. Issues hidden from both client and counsellor at the time of assessment will hopefully emerge at a later point and can be dealt with. Where the situation is known at the time of assessment to the client, but not to the counsellor, this will lead to the counsellor making a reassessment of the situation.

Some clients will not relate certain aspects of their difficulties because the counsellor has not asked the kinds of questions at assessment that would bring these to light. The style of questions discussed in the last chapter should lead to the disclosure of any relevant history. However, certain clients may have obscure reasons for construing that what they were asked did not specifically relate to the facts that only emerge at a later date. For example, a client, when asked whether he had ever been to his GP with anxiety, said that he had not. What emerged in later sessions showed that this was not the case, but the man thought that it 'did not count' because he had not been prescribed any treatment for the problem. A question at assessment asking whether the client knows of anything the counsellor has not asked about which may be relevant can be a useful safeguard against not having all the information that the client believes to be relevant. Some methods of counselling include assessment questionnaires; examples of this are behavioural counselling, cognitive-analytic therapy (CAT) and Lazarus' life history questionnaire (Lazarus, 1989). Some of these may bring to light medical or psychiatric issues that might otherwise remain unknown.

This does not deal, though, with the situation which can result from the counsellor being remiss in asking the right questions and the client being genuinely ignorant of the implications of their medical or psychiatric history or current diagnosis. Such eventualities will need some reassessment from the counsellor. The reassessment may be minor in nature, leading to little or no change in the direction that the counselling takes. At the other extreme it may lead to the possibility of counselling being considered inappropriate and consequently terminated. Where this needs to happen, it is crucial that, if at all possible, the counselling does not suddenly stop without the opportunity for the client to resolve dependency or other areas that may have arisen as a result of the sessions so far.

Where there has been some deliberate withholding or misleading on the part of the client, the situation needs to be approached differently. If a client appears to have acted deceptively it is easy to react angrily and look to terminate the counselling contract immediately, but this may be unduly punitive. It is important to elicit the reason why the client has pursued this particular course of action. The roots will often be in some kind of anxiety or fear, such as that disclosure will lead to help not being offered.

*Jane came for counselling asking for help with her sexual difficulties with her husband. Several sessions passed before she told the counsellor of her leukaemia and her fears that she would never see her young children grow up. This then became the central focus of the work with the counsellor, who judged that this was far too difficult an area to broach until Jane had firmly established a trust in the counselling relationship. At a later point*

*the original presenting problem, together with other issues, were
also worked with and understood in terms of the effects of chronic
illness and anticipation of loss.*


## Dilemmas Arising Particularly in Medical Settings

Those working in medical settings will face particular issues. For
example, the counsellor must be aware of the potential of being
drawn inappropriately into a disagreement between the client and
his practitioner about treatment of a concurrent medical or psychiatric condition. Where the counsellor takes up matters with the
practitioner it is important to be clear that this is an appropriate
response based on a sound professional judgement and not a
response to a client's anxieties, distortion of the facts or bullying
of the counsellor. Another dilemma arises when information has
been passed on with the referral that causes difficulties for the
counsellor in her ongoing work with the client. An example of
this is a definite or speculative diagnosis of illness in the client
about which the counsellor has not been informed. At the
extreme, the counsellor may be aware that the client most likely
has a limited life expectancy, a situation that the person has not
been informed about or does not understand.

In such situations it may be difficult for the counsellor to deal
with the material that the client brings except as seen in the
context of knowledge that is denied to the client. There may be
an additional pressure if the counsellor disagrees with the reasons
for withholding the information from the patient. In the end, the
only satisfactory solution to this problem is for counsellors in
medical settings to ensure that a referral system is set up which
avoids their knowing certain compromising facts about the
referred person. It is hoped that the counsellor will also have the
opportunity within the team to express her views about the way
information about patients' diagnoses is handled within the
organisation, and is entitled to expect respect for her views on
what should be disclosed to patients. The referring practitioners
may need to be educated by counsellors about the nature of their
work in order to understand that such matters are fundamental
and that the counsellor is not being too fussy or unreasonable.
Counsellors may need to consider making it clear that they are not
prepared to withhold information from their clients.

*Tom was referred to the practice counsellor for help with his anxiety. The counsellor was told by the GP that Tom had been treated for cancer and that his life expectancy was limited, but that he had not been told of the exact nature of his condition. As counselling progressed it became clear that Tom had not guessed the seriousness of his illness, and this caused increasing discomfort for the counsellor in having important knowledge about the client of which he seemed to be unaware. This led the counsellor to exchange views with the referring GP about whether to inform such patients more fully and to emphasise the importance of counsellors not being privy to important knowledge about clients that patients do not themselves have.*

Dilemmas can also operate in the opposite direction, when the client passes on information to the counsellor which is hidden from the referring practitioner. For example, the client may reveal that she is not taking prescribed medication and even that she is misleading her practitioner about this. By such a disclosure the counsellor may be placed in an ethical dilemma where there is a conflict between the counsellor's commitment to confidentiality about client material and his responsibility towards the organisation in terms of its wider duty of care to patients.

*John saw his GP about feeling depressed and the GP prescribed an anti-depressant and also referred him to the practice counsellor. During one of the sessions he revealed to the counsellor that he was using various illegal substances, a fact that he had not revealed to the GP. The counsellor was worried about how these might interact with the prescribed medication, but also concerned about confidentiality. However, in the end she felt that John's interest were best served by discussing her worries with the GP and told him that she was going to have to do this.*

There may also be inappropriate pressure brought on counsellors to disclose any information that might be helpful to others within the practice or unit in their treatment of the client. Again, education of the other professionals about the nature of the counselling contract is important, and they need to be convinced that such a passage of information is not in the long-term interests of their patients as it would eventually undermine the whole basis of the counselling. The question of who has access to the counsellor's records needs to be clear. These ethical problems are further discussed in Chapter 5.

There are other problems that may occur for those who work in medical settings as counselling progresses. Sometimes, as material is uncovered, clients will make more demands on carers, including the counsellor's colleagues. This may lead to some unpopularity, or questioning of the effectiveness of counselling. These kinds of dynamics can be further exacerbated by clients who try to play fellow professionals off against one another, especially where there are divisions to widen. Some benefit may be gained from an understanding of the dynamics of organisations, and by working out the dynamics within the counsellor's team. Clearly, it is most beneficial to have a team that supports and backs up one another to the benefit of patients, but where this ideal is not operating the counsellor will be helped in containing the situation by a clear understanding of the problem.

### Dilemmas Arising Particularly in Non-medical Settings

When medical or psychiatric concerns arise in the course of counselling those working in non-medical settings may feel particularly vulnerable. Ideally, counsellors should have easy access to medical advice, but this may not always be possible to establish. The range of the impact of the emergence of medical and psychiatric problems can be very wide, from the addition of a minor factor to the person's problems to an immediate suspension of counselling, as when a client is unexpectedly hospitalised. One common consequence will be a need to encourage the client to seek advice, probably from his GP. As part of this, the counsellor may judge it necessary to liaise with and work alongside the GP or other medical professionals. Clients' attitudes to such developments will be varied and unpredictable. Those who have shown a co-operative approach to the counselling may suddenly dig their heels in at the prospect of their GPs being contacted or the counsellor's communicating with another professional with whom the client is involved.

*Sue came for help with her relationship with her partner, with whom she had conflicts over his work and the way they should deal with the children. During one of the sessions she described symptoms which she understood as a kind of anxiety attack. However, the counsellor did not think these sounded like the usual kind of panic or anxiety attack and suggested that she visit her GP. The result of this visit was the diagnosis of a minor heart problem for which medication was needed.*

Some clients whose attitude to the sessions has been characterised by resistance may become unexpectedly compliant. The reasons for this, and other reactions, will only be discovered by exploring the meaning of the situation for the client and it will be necessary to work out an appropriate course of action with the client. In doing this the counsellor should aim for a co-operative approach with both clients and other professionals, but must also be prepared for the possibility of confrontation and conflict with either or both. Obviously, it is only in extreme situations that counsellors will contact someone's medical practitioner without the permission of a client, or carry on with counselling in the face of opposition from such a practitioner, but occasionally a counsellor may become convinced that a client's best interests will be served by these kinds of actions. Counsellors will inevitably find these situations arouse strong feelings, and must be careful not to confuse acting in the client's interest with defending their professional power or responding to having their professional hackles raised.

## Managing Gaps

Another consequence of the emergence of a medical or psychiatric issue may be the re-assessment of the appropriateness of counselling or of its place in the overall treatment of the client. This is especially so when the regularity of the sessions is subject to interruptions by periods of illness or hospitalisation. If it can be coped with in the counsellor's work pattern, to continue to accommodate the client as far as possible can often be a valuable contribution to the resolution of her emotional problems. Conversely, the perception of abandonment during a period of illness or adversity can have the opposite effect. During gaps, contact by telephone or letter can be valuable, if this is possible. In the case of psychiatric hospitalisation, where the value of ongoing counselling and continuity of care is usually appreciated, arrangements may be made for the client to continue the counselling or, if she is unable to leave the hospital alone, a room may be made available on the ward. Exceptionally, an escort may be provided to enable the client to continue seeing the counsellor in the usual setting.

One question that can arise is whether the counsellor should visit in hospital. It can often seem a natural response and a good way of ensuring continuity of contact. However, there are a number of possible pitfalls with such visits. For example, the confidentiality of the relationship may be compromised, not only to others who may be visiting the client, but also to hospital staff and other patients with whom the client may have become friendly. Additionally, the counsellor will usually risk having to interact with the client's family or friends who may already be with the person, or who may arrive during the course of the counsellor's visit. With such people present it will also be impossible for the sensitive issues that have been part of the counselling to be aired.

Such discussions may be impossible in any event, due to lack of privacy from other patients, or the difficulty of managing a completely different setting. The counsellor may easily find herself part of an uncomfortable conversation consisting only of social niceties and awkward silences which later proves to be counter-productive when counselling is able to resume in its proper setting. There may be exceptions, though, and these are likely to be in situations where the client has no family or friends, or is too far from them to receive visitors. The value of the support that may be offered in such instances may be judged to outweigh the possible disadvantages. Another exception may be when a counsellor has been working with someone with a terminal illness who has now become too ill to attend for counselling.

Sometimes the pressure on the counsellor's time, the length of the gaps involved or the nature of the client's condition may make it impossible to continue. In such instances it is important to be aware of the client's feelings of rejection and accompanying frustration and anger that may be aroused by such an outcome, and the need to try to find alternative sources of help that may still be available to the client in the new situation.

*Glen, a student in his twenties, had not been in counselling long before cancer was diagnosed. His illness required periods of chemotherapy, during which he felt too ill to attend sessions. This was very disruptive, but as the counsellor could accommodate these gaps into his schedule, the sessions continued through this period of treatment when Glen was well enough to attend. After the end of chemotherapy, weekly sessions were re-established and Glen found these helpful in coming to terms with his illness as well as continuing to work on the original areas of difficulty.*

## The Dying Client

Where a counsellor is working with a client who is dying, this brings particular pressures on the counselling situation. When problems unrelated to illness are involved, it will bring a sense of urgency to the counselling, as both counsellor and client recognise that the time available to work on difficulties is almost certain to be limited. Whilst the probing and uncovering of conflicts might be possible and appropriate in the early stage of terminal illness, Levy (1990) suggests that, in the later stages, the fostering of denial and other defences may be adaptive for the client where they do not prevent necessary planning or communication. It will be helpful to focus on areas which can result in improvement or maintenance of the person's quality of life and decisions about whether the person will die at home, in hospital or in a hospice. When the working situation is one where it is common for clients to be approaching death, such as a hospice, particular demands are made on a counsellor who may find herself in a continual process of bereavement. Where possible it is advisable that the counsellor's caseload should be balanced by clients who are at a very different point in their lives, and supervisors can help counsellors to be aware of this need.

More commonly, clients who are dying will be encountered only occasionally and bring an impact in a different way. Counsellors may find themselves suddenly confronted with their own mortality in an unexpected way, and may find it hard to give their full attention to the clients' material in sessions. Levy says that 'Situations in which the therapist feels helpless to alter any final outcome, and those that confront the therapist with his or her own death, may precipitate intense reactions and have profound consequences for the therapist's own life' (1990: 209). The help and support of the supervisor can be crucial when a client raises strong anxieties in the counsellor. Where counselling is brought to a premature end by a client's death, the sense of loss felt by the counsellor can also be usefully worked on in supervision. The appropriateness or otherwise of attending the funeral will depend on the particular circumstances of the counselling and the wishes of the family. Where they know about the counselling and its importance to the person they will generally be keen for the counsellor to attend. In other situations there may be ambivalence or opposition, with a resultant difficulty in denying a request to attend if one comes from the counsellor. Where the counsellor judges that attending the funeral is not appropriate or wise, then it may compound the counsellor's difficulties in coming to terms with the death.

## The Counsellor's Own Illness

A subject that also arouses strong feelings of vulnerability in the counsellor is the issue of her own illnesses. This perhaps accounts for the fact that it is not often addressed and very little has been written on it. In this account we are indebted to the review article by Counselman and Alonso (1993).

In general, professional helpers prefer to be in the role of givers rather than receivers. This can be reinforced by clients, who often prefer to see their counsellors as invulnerable. There is a tendency for the young to see illness as a problem of the old, as though young people do not become ill. There is evidence that some older counsellors do not address it either and seem to become caught up in the idea that they are going to carry on for ever.

It is important, in general, for a counsellor to enjoy good health to the extent that she does not regularly need to have periods away from the work with clients, as counselling differs from virtually all other professions in the lack of an available substitute. An exception might be where a counsellor has a suitable colleague, and it might be useful for them to see the client in the counsellor's absence. Preferably, the colleague should be familiar with the client and well versed in the problems that might arise surrounding the leave caused by the counsellor's illness.

Someone considering training for long-term, particularly psychodynamic, counselling and who generally has several weeks a year off work ill or receiving medical treatment, either because of an ongoing chronic illness, or susceptibility to whatever viruses are going round, should seriously consider whether it is the right occupation to enter. This may seem harsh, but many, if not most, clients have suffered from inconsistent or absent parents and it is unhelpful if this is reinforced by the counsellor's absences. With other approaches, such as cognitive-behavioural counselling, or where short-term or non-regular sessions are offered, such considerations may not arise in the same way.

## Managing the Counsellor's Own Illness with Clients

To some extent the circumstances of the counsellor's absence will determine the impact on the counselling. If the counsellor is undergoing planned surgery where the date is known by clients well in advance, this will be very different from the counsellor being taken ill very suddenly and as a result becoming immediately unavailable to clients for a period of time which is unknown.

The particular circumstances will not in themselves determine the outcome, for example, because a period of notice needs to be utilised by the counsellor in the work with the client. Also, where clients have no particular problem with life's unpredictability, they may be able to weather the sudden absence without too much difficulty. The crucial element is probably the impact of the event on the trust of the client, both the trust in the counsellor and in the counselling process.

Therefore the impact of the counsellor's illness on the counselling depends very much on how it is handled by the counsellor. Illness challenges a person's defences against neediness and helplessness and it may be hard for the counsellor to give proper attention to the client's concerns about the illness.

*Pamela was working full-time as a counsellor when it became clear that she needed a hysterectomy. As this could be performed in a planned way rather than as an emergency, this enabled her to prepare her clients for an absence of six to eight weeks. A feature of this was the different reactions she had from clients. Some became very concerned about her health and pressed for further details about her condition. Pamela was rather shocked by one client who seemed to have no concern for her and was angry at being abandoned. Discussing this in supervision made her more aware of her vulnerability and a tendency to look to her clients for concerned support, which she recognised was important to resist. In supervision Pamela also identified a small group*

---

**Client Concerns about Counsellor Illness**

1  Security
   Is the illness serious?
   Might the counsellor have to cancel sessions?
   Will the counsellor die?

2  Fear about damaging the counsellor
   Have I in some way caused this?
   Should I offer to discontinue the session because the counsellor
     may be in too much pain/discomfort to carry on today?
   Are my problems too much for her when she is unwell?

3  Anger
   The counsellor should not be vulnerable.
   The counsellor should be strong for me.
   How can he help me when he cannot sort out his own life?

---

*of clients who were particularly in need and would benefit from
the opportunity to contact another counsellor in the organisation
if the need arose during her absence.*

Where absences occur the counsellor must be ready to deal not
only with clients' positive concern, but also with anger and other
negative feelings. The latter are likely to be difficult to handle,
especially if the illness has been traumatic or distressing for the
counsellor. It can sometimes be hard to continue addressing the
client's concerns and not to retaliate from a place of hurt.

It is not an uncommon experience for most counsellors to have
days when they feel ill or tired, but consider that they are well
enough to carry on working. On such days comments can come
from clients, such as 'You're looking tired today' or 'Are you ill?'
When these sorts of comments are made, to give full explanations
or to ignore or deny the comments is not normally helpful
because it leads to a focus on the counsellor's problems or
defensiveness. Generally, it is best to deal with the issue first in
terms of the client's own concerns which might lie behind the
comment, and this is especially so if the counsellor feels that she
is looking ill or tired!

Where the counsellor recognises that she is looking below par,
it is best also to address the reality of the situation in addition to

referring it to previous client material. A suitable response would be one that shows appreciation of the client's concern, but also gives reassurance about the counsellor's ability to work with the client in that day's session. The question arises concerning when the counsellor is ill with a bad cold, flu or other infectious illness. A consideration over and above the counsellor's desire to work is the risk of transmitting infections to clients, especially if there are those who are particularly vulnerable.

The counsellor needs to judge according to his work situation and clients at the time how much to make the decision himself or how much to leave clients to judge whether they wish to take the risk of catching the illness. An important area is how the counsellor looks after his health, and he should not fall prey to exaggerated feelings of responsibility or distorted ideas of indispensability and continue to work when really he should be off sick. Counsellors find this area difficult, and discussion in supervision about when taking time off is appropriate may be needed to obtain a proper perspective.

## Managing More Serious Illness Situations with Clients

Where more serious and long-term illness is involved, the amount of information given will be partly dependent on the counsellor's theoretical orientation. For example, a psychodynamic counsellor working with transference may choose to withhold more than a cognitive-behavioural counsellor. All counsellors, though, need to have a flexibility based on the needs of their clients. A situation that counsellors in private practice may face is a reluctance on the part of colleagues to refer to someone who is suffering illness. This may lead to the decline of the counsellor's practice and consequent economic difficulties and problems in relationships with colleagues.

Another painful issue is the recognition that some medical and psychiatric conditions should lead counsellors to consider stopping their practice. This may be either because the person is not physically well enough to work, or because she is not able to counsel effectively as a result of her psychological state. Counsellors need to be aware of the relevant parts of their code of ethics – see also Bond (1993a) for a discussion of the ethics of counsellors' limits of competence. The question of whether the ill counsellor continues to practise is different from those who have every reason to believe they are going to recover compared with those who know that the chances are that they will not. In many instances it will be too much to ask that the client works with the knowledge that his counsellor is likely to die in the near future.

The danger in the ill counsellor continuing to work is that she may project her own feelings about her illness onto clients. The chronically ill counsellor is likely to withdraw emotionally from clients. There may also be a difficulty of envy of her clients who are seen as 'well'. In all these difficulties it is important for supervisors to help counsellors and for counsellors to remain open to such help. The challenge for the psychodynamic counsellor is to remain neutral to clients' expressions about the counsellor's illness in the sense of treating all comments and responses with equal respect and interest. For other perspectives a more directive approach to the situation will be more appropriate. In any event, the counsellor needs to work through with each client what the illness means for them. Again, the extent to which this is carried through will depend somewhat on the counsellor's theoretical orientation.

Where denial is used as a defence by a counsellor against the seriousness of a situation, or certain psychiatric conditions are involved, the counsellor's colleagues may have to take on a difficult task of informing or advising the counsellor who may not be aware of, or may not want to acknowledge, the growing deficits in his abilities. In any event, the counsellor needs to look to trusted colleagues, supervisors and possibly his own counselling or therapy in making both professional and personal decisions in such difficult circumstances. Although it may appear morbid or extreme, all counsellors need to think about what would happen in the case of their illness, unavoidable absence or sudden death and to make whatever plans might be necessary. For those working in an organisation where there are other counsellors, this may simply be a matter of checking that there are clear lines of responsibility which would ensure that clients were contacted and offered suitable alternative help.

For those in more isolated work settings and single-handed private practice it is advisable to make a will to deal with such an eventuality, including the appointment of a suitably qualified executor. This should safeguard not only what happens to clients, but also the confidentiality of notes and so on. Guidelines for drawing up such a will are included on pages 130–1 as part of the appendices.

## Visible Disabilities and Disfigurements

If the counsellor has a visible disability or disfigurement this will raise similar, but also separate, concerns to those discussed above. Some disabilities will arouse protective concerns in clients that may make it difficult for them to see the counsellor as robust enough to deal with their problems or able to cope with, for example, expressions of anger. Others may raise fundamental concerns about the counsellor's ability to counsel adequately. For example, faced with a counsellor who is blind, the client may feel that the counselling will not be satisfactory because of the importance of being 'seen' and of expressions and reactions being noted visually as well as in other ways. A noticeable facial disfigurement may make it difficult for the client to look at the counsellor.

In these circumstances it is almost inevitable that contradictory feelings will be aroused in the client. On the one hand, there may be concern and sympathy for the counsellor, and on the other, anger and resentment that the counsellor and the counselling is somehow less than perfect. It is important that counsellors are aware of the kinds of reactions that any disabilities or disfigurements that they have are likely to arouse in clients. They then need to work out the appropriate way in which these could be responded to within the theoretical framework they utilise in their work.

## The Pregnant Counsellor

Although we would want strongly to resist any view of pregnancy that leads it to be seen as illness or medicalises it, it does impact on the counsellor and the counselling in similar ways in terms of preoccupation and gaps away from work. There will also be some medical aspects to pregnancy, if only that the counsellor will need to attend ante-natal appointments and classes which will probably cut across some appointments with clients. There will also be a period of maternity leave which will follow a similar pattern to that of planned surgery, but with rather a different potential impact on the counselling, as we shall see below. Where there are complications to the counsellor's pregnancy there will be a correspondingly greater impact on her work. These may range from a degree of preoccupied anxiety about the way that the pregnancy is going to a period of prolonged hospitalisation.

Additionally, some counsellors will be trying to become pregnant without success, and a proportion of these will go on to various forms of fertility treatment and varying degrees of preoccupation with the difficulties which they are experiencing. Unfortunately, some counsellors' pregnancies will end in miscarriage, with consequent physical and emotional impact. Other counsellors may find themselves in the position of considering, or having, an abortion. We need to consider the effects of all these scenarios on the counselling.

## Disclosure

Where things are hidden, there will not be the opportunity for their impact to be discussed in the counselling. Just because the realities are not openly acknowledged, though, does not mean that they do not have effects on the counselling. At some level the client may pick up the counsellor's preoccupation, anxiety or pain, and the counsellor needs to be aware that this may happen and be prepared to deal with it. The degree to which self-disclosure is considered inappropriate will vary according to theoretical orientation, but the counsellor needs to ensure that the client does not come to the conclusion that he is the cause of these feelings, or that he is wrong in his conclusions about how the counsellor is feeling. If either of these does happen, then the client comes to have a more distorted view of his relationship with the world. The counsellor must be able to validate the client's sense of what is happening to the counsellor without making inappropriate disclosures or making the client feel responsible for looking after the counsellor.

## Routine Pregnancy

In the usual course of events the pregnant counsellor will be faced with the disruption of ante-natal appointments followed by either leaving work or a period of maternity leave. Where maternity leave is taken the use of an alternative counsellor to bridge the gap might be usefully considered (McCarty et al., 1986). Routine ante-natal appointments will generally be on the same morning or afternoon of the week and so the same clients

---

**Possible Issues Arising for Clients with Pregnant Counsellors**

- Envy of the counsellor
- Envy of the unborn baby
- Anger, or even rage, that the counsellor has 'chosen' to prioritise care for another over the client
- Anxiety about being abandoned
- Identification with the unborn baby
- Hurt at the counsellor's being seen as 'preferring' the baby to the client
- Care about and/or love for the counsellor and the unborn baby
- Linking in with own or partner's pregnancies
- Feelings of envy of counsellor's partner
- Triggering of sexual feelings towards counsellor
- Concern about the counsellor's well-being
- Possibility of a premature end to the counselling
- Possibility of a gap in the counselling, the length of which may not be known until after the birth

---

may face disruption on each occasion. Where the pregnancy is planned it may be possible for the counsellor to discover well in advance when in the week these appointments are likely to fall and for her to do a certain amount of forward planning. One decision to be made will be at what point to tell ongoing clients. This should probably be just before it becomes physically obvious, but clients may pre-empt this by asking before that point and the counsellor should be prepared for this. At the point of disclosure there is likely to be an immediate intensification in the relationship between the counsellor and the client.

These possibilities need to be explored and worked through without making assumptions about which ones are relevant to particular clients and which may be the most important to them. Clues about important areas can undoubtedly be obtained from the counsellor's understanding of her clients' problems and the issues that have arisen in the counselling up to the point that the counsellor's pregnancy becomes an open issue with the client.

*Andrea had been in counselling for a number of months before the counsellor became pregnant. The nature of the work was long-term and needed to continue beyond the counsellor's mater-nity leave. However, Andrea found it very difficult to discuss the*

---

**Possible Issues Arising for Pregnant Counsellors in Relation to Clients**

- Preoccupation with being pregnant
- Feelings of vulnerability
- Preoccupation with concern about the unborn baby
- Difficulty of coping with clients' negative feelings about the pregnancy
- Ambivalence about continuing to work whilst being pregnant
- Uncertainty about whether to leave work or, if maternity leave is taken, at what point to return

---

*impending break in counselling or the possibility of resuming sessions afterwards. In exploring this it became clear that she was experiencing feelings of being replaced by the baby, and was finding it hard to believe that the counsellor would ever be available for her in the same way again. Andrea was angry about the pregnancy, and about the possibility that the counsellor might have more children in the future, but found it hard to express this, the more so because she was a mother herself. The situation was further complicated by Andrea bringing various gifts of knitwear to the sessions which her mother had knitted for the baby. It emerged that Andrea did not really want to bring these and saw them as an intrusion into her counselling. The counsellor understood them as a message from Andrea's mother that she feared being seen as a bad mother and this was a way of telling the counsellor that she was a good mother.*

## Issues for the Supervisor

Supervisors of counsellors will need to address a wider range of the points we have covered than an individual practitioner will encounter. Therefore it is incumbent on the supervisor to have given some thought to the whole range of matters that may arise for his supervisees. It is also important for supervisors to realise that counsellors may be unaware of the implications of some of the situations we have covered. Consequently it may be necessary to be on the look-out for potential medical and psychiatric dilemmas and where necessary tease these out from the material that the supervisee is presenting.

A difficulty for supervisors is that they are dealing with client situations second hand. This gives less direct access to information about and from clients and also less access to taking direct action where this is appropriate. Supervisors are very dependent on what supervisees bring and what action they may be prepared to consider in relation to their clients. It is important to have a clear idea of areas that can be left to the supervisee's discretion. There will be other situations where the supervisor needs to give clear advice or specific direction, and rare occasions where the supervisor may have to consider taking some responsibility to act directly herself (see Chapter 5 on ethical issues).

Sometimes medical and psychiatric conditions in clients will create undue concern or anxiety in counsellors, and supervisors at times will need to help supervisees contain their feelings. There may also be complex ethical issues which the supervisor can assist the counsellor to resolve. These may in turn raise ethical, and even legal, dilemmas for the supervisee which will be further discussed in Chapter 5. Counsellors will need help to enable them not to take precipitous action where this is not needed and which may even be detrimental to the counselling process. Although it is unrealistic to expect that supervisors can be authoritative sources of expertise on illness, drugs and allied matters, it is important that they are experienced and competent in the aspects of medical and psychiatric knowledge that fall within the counselling arena.

It is important that counsellors who act as supervisors have regular supervision for this work. It is also vital that supervisors have access to advice from medical practitioners and mental health professionals that is reliable and readily accessible. At present the responsibilities of supervisors in relation to their supervisees' clients is rather unclear, but it is evident that there is some responsibility that may extend beyond working with the supervisee if the supervisor believes that there is negligence on the part of the counsellor. It is also apparent that the supervisor does not discharge her responsibility by merely discontinuing supervision in response to a counsellor's negligence or unprofessional behaviour.

## Conclusion

The counsellor must be prepared for medical and psychiatric conditions to emerge in clients during the course of counselling.

The counsellor needs to have this possibility in mind during his work and maximise the possibility of detecting medical and psychiatric conditions at an early stage. These conditions in clients will sometimes be quite disruptive of the counselling process, because they disrupt the nature of the work or the regularity of sessions, or both. The counsellor needs constructive strategies to deal with these.

The counsellor also needs to realise that she can become ill and must have ways of managing the impact of this on her work. In rare situations the counsellor may have to come to the difficult decision of retiring from counselling work. Some of the same issues, and others, arise in the case of pregnancy in the counsellor. Supervisors need to be consulted about all these matters and themselves need the training and experience to help supervisees in this aspect of their work.

# 3

# *Medical Conditions and their Treatment in Relation to Counselling*

A useful distinction is made in clinical medical practice between the signs and symptoms of disease. *Signs* are those things about a patient which others can detect with their own senses: pallor, abnormal behaviour or a heart murmur, for example. *Symptoms* are those experiences which a patient reports, such as pain, hallucinations or diarrhoea.

A client may describe various symptoms to the counsellor, either at initial presentation or during the counselling process. In addition, the counsellor may notice various signs in the client. Either way, the counsellor may have the problem of deciding whether to advise the client to seek medical advice. This decision is often problematic because many symptoms may result either from an underlying biophysical process or from psychosocial distress. A biophysical process is one in which physical changes may be measured within the body. Such changes are often referred to as pathological. Psychosocial processes, on the other hand, are those involving thoughts, feelings and relationships with others. Much emotional distress is, of course, a reflection of painful psychosocial processes.

To take a specific example, a headache may reflect pathological changes in the head, or a sense of being trapped and powerless in an unhappy relationship. In the first instance, medical referral could lead to early treatment and might even save the patient's life. In the absence of physical pathology, however, medical consultation and investigation are likely to deflect attention from important psychosocial issues. At best this may delay the counselling process, at worse it can lead to a disabling belief that symptoms are due to as-yet-undiagnosed physical pathology (Grol, 1981).

Later in this chapter, we will describe a number of common symptoms which may arise either from psychosocial distress or from biophysical disease. We will offer pointers to those features of each symptom which might suggest a biophysical disease process. First, however, the relationship between *psychosocial* processes and *biophysical* conditions requires further discussion. Although it may be convenient to regard an illness as primarily psychosocial or as primarily biophysical in origin, and it is often useful to do so, the majority of illnesses involve both biophysical and psychosocial factors. Underlying the symptoms of migraine, for example, are the biophysical processes of constriction of blood vessels within the skull, followed by dilatation of blood vessels in the scalp. However, an episode of migraine may be associated with powerful emotions such as anxiety or anger, and may follow an upsetting experience at home or at work. Furthermore, the decision by the migraine sufferer to treat himself, to seek medical attention, or to discuss his symptoms with a counsellor will also reflect a number of psychosocial processes. Prominent amongst these is likely to be the way in which he frames his symptoms: as an unavoidable aspect of his personality perhaps; as a physical disease; or as a consequence of an unhappy marriage. These attributions will be informed by his view of the world and his place within it, by the views of others in his life, and by his previous experiences of seeking medical or psychological help (Usherwood, 1990).

Thus both psychosocial and biophysical processes may need to be considered in seeking to understand why a particular person reports a particular symptom or symptoms in a particular way and at a particular time. One way of understanding the psychosocial processes is in terms of the client's *health beliefs*. The client will have a set of beliefs about his symptoms which reflect his cultural background, his previous experiences, and the views expressed by others in his life. These beliefs will inform any fears or concerns that he has about his symptoms, his behaviour in relation to his symptoms, and his hopes and expectations concerning the results of that behaviour (Pendleton et al., 1984). Furthermore, these beliefs are unlikely to be fixed, but will change and evolve to incorporate the client's interpretations of his ongoing experiences and the conversations he has with significant others – including his counsellor and his doctor (Tuckett et al., 1985).

A second way of understanding the ways in which a person interprets, feels and behaves in relation to perceived symptoms is in terms of his *unconscious processes*. These are likely to be particularly significant in the context of interpersonal illness-related behaviour. Thus, the issues of why a client tells the counsellor about a particular symptom, and why he does so in a particular way, may sometimes be understood best from a psychodynamic perspective (Passmore, 1973). Other ways of understanding some examples of illness behaviour are in terms of *'compensation neurosis'*, *factitious symptoms* and *secondary gain*. These issues are discussed later in this chapter, in the section on back pain.

Although the remainder of this chapter will be concerned largely with physical symptoms, underlying diseases, and guidance on when to refer for medical assessment, the counsellor whose client reports a physical problem must do more than merely decide whether to advise medical consultation. While evaluating the client's symptoms she should also consider and reflect on the client's associated health beliefs and the possible hidden or unconscious motivations for his behaviour. The counsellor must also think about the implications of her own words and actions in relation to these factors, and bear in mind that, whatever she says or does is likely to affect the psychosocial aspects of the illness in some way.

Before going on to consider specific medical conditions, it is worth making the general point that almost any symptom, and many diseases, can represent an adverse effect of prescribed medication that is being taken for another purpose. Conversely, any medication that is prescribed for physical or psychological illness may have unintended adverse effects. A lengthy account of the adverse effects of prescribed drugs would be out of place in this book. However, the counsellor should always bear in mind the possibility of a drug effect whenever a client describes untoward symptoms. The British National Formulary and the ABPI Data Sheet Compendium are invaluable sources of information about intended and unintended effects of drugs, and are revised annually.

Finally, it would be impossible in a book of this length to describe every symptom and disease that a counsellor might meet in his or her career. It is not even possible to provide a comprehensive account of the clinical features, treatment options and implications for the counselling process of all the commoner medical conditions. Instead, in this chapter we have attempted to include a variety of common problems, and a few that are less common, with the aim of highlighting important lessons and illustrating key issues. We have included references in the text in order to point the reader towards more detailed and comprehensive discussions of many of these topics. At the end of the chapter we list those questions that the counsellor should ask herself whenever a client discloses a new symptom or other medical problem, and we give some general advice on when to refer for medical assessment.

### Headache

We have already used this symptom as an example of a problem which may indicate psychosocial distress, biophysical pathology or both, and which may benefit from one or both of counselling and medical intervention. Most people experience headaches at some stage in their lives. Probably the commonest type of headache is the so-called *tension headache*. This is typically described as feeling like a pressure on top of the head or a band around the head. It may be experienced for hours, days or weeks at a time, and relief from analgesics such as paracetamol or aspirin may be only partial or short-lived. Tension headache is thought to arise from contraction in muscles of the forehead, back of the head and back of the neck. It may be associated with worrying or distressing life events and may be accompanied by a low mood and other symptoms of a depressive illness (see Chapter 4). Resolution of the depression is then usually associated with relief from the headache.

Another very common cause of headache in adults is *migraine*. This may occur at any age but usually begins between ages 10 and 30 years. It is less common after the age of 50 years. Women suffer migraine more often than men and over 50 per cent of people who suffer with migraine know of others in the family who have the same condition. Migraine occurs in episodes. Typically, the headache is preceded by an aura. This is a period of depression, irritability, restlessness or visual disturbance. These symptoms may disappear as the headache starts, or may continue. The headache often starts in one temple and may generalise to both sides, but it may be felt on both sides from the beginning. Nausea, vomiting and abdominal pain may accompany the headache. A common symptom is to find bright lights unpleasant. Untreated episodes may last for hours or days, and the sufferer may feel poorly for anything up to a few days after an attack. Migraine symptoms usually follow the same pattern in any individual, except that one-sided headaches may not always be on the same side. Sometimes triggers can be identified that start episodes in a particular person: certain foods, alcohol, caffeine, hunger, fatigue, anxiety, anger and strong emotions are common. Women may find they are more prone to migraine about the time of their periods.

A less common, but important, cause of headache is *physical trauma*. Headache following a blow to the head is not unexpected, and neither is tender, painful bruising located at the site of the blow and lasting for a week or two afterwards. However, a few people describe headache that persists for weeks, months or years following the original injury. The pain may be localised or generalised, and may vary over time in intensity, frequency and duration. It may be made worse by sudden movements of the head and by alcohol. It is often worse at times of strongly felt emotion, and may be associated with symptoms of depression such as irritability, inability to concentrate and difficulty in sleeping. The headache may be associated with feelings of dizziness or vertigo, and on occasion may mimic tension headache or migraine.

Headache can be a very worrying symptom and can raise concerns about life-threatening disease. However, serious disease is unlikely in a client who has typical symptoms of tension headache or migraine and who describes similar experiences in the past. On the other hand, *medical referral should be considered if the headache is of recent onset, is unusually severe or disabling, wakes the client up at night, or follows a recent head injury. Headaches accompanied by severe visual disturbance or by symptoms other than those*

**described as typical of tension headache or migraine should also lead the counsellor to consider medical referral.**

### Tremor and Other Abnormal Movements

Tremor is defined as a rapid, rhythmically repetitive movement which tends to be consistent in pattern, amplitude and frequency (Walton, 1989). A fine, rapid tremor is a well-known sign of anxiety. However, it may also be seen in a heavy user of alcohol who has not had a drink for a few hours or days, in people who are particularly sensitive to caffeine in tea or coffee, and in association with certain prescribed drugs. One drug that often causes fine tremor is *lithium*, used in the treatment of bipolar affective disorder and other psychiatric conditions (see Table 4.8 in Chapter 4).

Tremor is also a feature of *hyperthyroidism*. Hyperthyroidism is sometimes known as *thyrotoxicosis*, and is due to overactivity of the thyroid gland. Other symptoms and signs of hyperthyroidism are *goitre* (swelling of the thyroid gland in the neck), exophthalmos (bulging of the eyes), nervousness, intolerance of heat, fatigue, increased appetite, weight loss and occasionally diarrhoea.

The latter symptoms are very similar to those of *generalised anxiety disorder*, and it is not always possible to distinguish the two conditions without a blood test or other investigations. **A client who describes symptoms of anxiety but who has goitre or exophthalmos should be referred for medical advice.**

*Benign essential tremor* is rather slower and usually affects the hands, head and voice. It is less marked or absent at rest and occurs during movement, especially during actions that require fine co-ordination. A person with this condition may find that she spills an over-full cup of tea while raising it to her lips. Anxiety and fatigue make benign essential tremor worse, and it tends to increase with age. It is sometimes mistakenly called senile tremor for this reason. In some people a small amount of alcohol markedly suppresses the tremor and occasionally this can lead to over-use. About 50 per cent of people with benign essential tremor have a family history of the condition, although it may not become apparent until later in life.

Tremor occurring at rest and diminishing during movement is typical of *Parkinson's disease* (Quinn, 1995). In the early stages of the disease it is often restricted to one hand and is sometimes described as 'pill-rolling' in nature. The tremor of Parkinson's disease is slower than the types of tremor already described, with a frequency of between three and five cycles per second. It is typically made worse by emotional tension and fatigue. Other features of Parkinson's disease are reduction in spontaneous movements, difficulty in initiating movements, and movements themselves being slow and somewhat clumsy. In the early stages of the condition, a person with Parkinson's disease is likely to be more concerned about akinesia than about the tremor. *Akinesia* is the name given to a combination of symptoms including slowness of intentional movement, poverty of spontaneous movement (such as smiling, or arm swinging while walking), difficulty initiating movements, and progressive fatiguing, especially of repetitive, alternating movements. Another common complaint is of a tendency to stumble. Parkinson's disease usually starts sometime after the age of 50 years, and is due to degeneration of cells in a part of the brain known as the *substantia nigra*. It gets progressively worse with time, and many people with the disease become depressed and may contemplate suicide.

Parkinsonism, in which the symptoms and signs of Parkinson's disease are caused by something other than degeneration of cells in the substantia nigra, may occur at any age. Prescribed drugs are a common cause of Parkinsonism, especially the *major tranquillisers* such as chlorpromazine and haloperidol (see Table 4.6).

Other causes of tremor are rare and are usually associated with additional signs and symptoms such that the person observing them in himself seeks medical help. This is also true of most of the other movement disorders, such as *myoclonus, chorea, athetosis* and *dystonia* (Walton, 1989). *Tics,* on the other hand, are not uncommon. They often occur in isolation, may start in childhood and may never have led to a medical consultation. Tics are brief, rapid, involuntary movements that can be simple or complex; they are stereotyped and repetitive but not rhythmic. Simple tics such as eye blinking or grunting often begin as nervous mannerisms in childhood or later and may disappear spontaneously. Complex tics often resemble fragments of normal behaviour. Although tics are involuntary, they can usually be suppressed for a variable amount of time.

The main cause of tics, other than simple tics of childhood, is *Tourette's syndrome.* This is characterised by multiple tics which begin in childhood and become more complex with age. The adult with Tourette's syndrome can typically describe or demonstrate several different types of tic, and occasionally exhibits *coprolalia*. This is a compulsion to utter short, obscene words or phrases. The syndrome may be associated with compulsive behaviour or a rigid personality. In his article 'Witty ticcy Ray' Sacks (1986: 87–96) gives a memorable description of the condition, although he tends to over-romanticise it. If marked, both the tics and the coprolalia can be severely disabling socially. Medication can be helpful in reducing the frequency of involuntary movements and utterances. *If the client has not sought medical advice, then the counsellor should consider raising this as an option.*

### Dyspnoea and Chest Pain

Dyspnoea, or shortness of breath, refers to the subjective experience of difficulty in breathing. It may be of long duration or recent onset and may be constant, slowly progressive, or fluctuating and episodic. Mild degrees of dyspnoea are experienced only on exertion, whilst more severe degrees may be experienced even at rest. Dyspnoea may be caused by almost any disease of the lungs and by many diseases of the heart. In the case of lung disease, it is often but not always accompanied by a cough. In the case of heart disease, it may be accompanied by a cough or by chest pain, or may occur alone. Other biophysical causes of dyspnoea include severe anaemia and kidney failure, but these are very rare.

Probably the commonest biophysical cause of dyspnoea is *asthma* (Pearson, 1990). Up to one-fifth of children have current or recent symptoms of asthma (Usherwood, 1987), and the disease is also common in adults. The symptoms of asthma are cough, wheeze, chest pain and dyspnoea. Symptoms usually occur in episodes, which may be brought about by triggers such as exertion, cigarette smoke or the common cold. Emotional upset may also act as a trigger in some people with asthma, but *emotional problems are not a cause of the disease itself*. Many people with asthma feel very stigmatised by their disease, and pessimistic about its prognosis. These attitudes tend to be more marked in people with more severe symptoms (Sibbald et al., 1988).

Dyspnoea can also be a feature of psychological illness. Two particular patterns stand out. In the first the client describes a sense of inadequacy of inspiration (breathing in) such that he occasionally has to take a deep breath in order to fill the lungs properly (Gardner and Bass, 1989). He may also describe or exhibit occasional sighs as he breathes out following a particularly deep inspiration. In addition, the client may describe pain in the chest, usually in localized areas at the front. The pain is often short-lasting, and may be described as sharp in quality. The client may exhibit a rather erratic respiratory cycle, particularly if his attention is drawn to his breathing. People with these symptoms are often worried about the possibility of heart disease, and may describe other symptoms of anxiety (see Table 4.3 in Chapter 4).

The second common pattern of dyspnoea associated with psychological problems is that of episodic *panic attacks*. These typically last a few minutes to an hour or two. During an attack, marked dyspnoea is associated with a sense of dread or terror, and often with palpitations, chest discomfort, uncontrollable shaking, and tingling or numbness around the mouth and in the fingers and toes. The person experiencing the attack may be convinced that she is going to die. Occasionally clients with the disordered respiratory pattern and sighing respiration described in the previous paragraph may exhibit panic attacks. Panic attacks are a feature of anxiety neurosis and may also occur in depressive illness (see Chapter 4).

Although the two patterns of dyspnoea described above typically reflect psychological disturbance, they may both on occasion be caused by biophysical disease such as asthma or heart problems. *If the client has not sought medical advice concerning these symptoms then the counsellor should consider referral,* particularly if the symptoms are of comparatively recent onset. Although in most instances no abnormalities of heart or lungs will be detected, serious or even life-threatening pathology will occasionally be found.

In addition to dyspnoea, many heart and lung diseases can cause chest pain. The commonest example due to heart disease is *angina*. This occurs in episodes that may last anything from less than a minute to the best part of an hour. Angina is usually described as tight, gripping or heavy in quality, occurring in the front of the chest and spreading into the neck, back or arms. Although it can occur at rest, an episode of angina usually starts during exertion. If the person stops what they are doing then the pain will slowly disappear. Appropriate medication will help it disappear more quickly; such medication is in the form of either tablets which are dissolved under the tongue, or a spray. Rarely a client with angina may develop an episode during a counselling session. If the pain does not rapidly and completely respond to the client's usual medication, or if the pain then recurs, you should not leave the client but should ***telephone for urgent medical advice, either from the client's general practitioner or another doctor. If such advice is not readily available, or if the client appears distressed or ill in any way, then send for an ambulance.***

Other diseases of the heart, and diseases of the lungs such as asthma, cancer, pneumonia and pleurisy, can cause chest pain of various descriptions. As indicated earlier in this section, chest pain may also be felt in the absence of evidence of biophysical disease. Such pain usually occurs in one or more localised areas, and is usually associated with local tenderness. A likely cause is prolonged contraction of the muscles of the chest wall in the area of the pain.

*In general, it is wise to assume that a client who describes pain in the chest has a significant medical problem until proved otherwise.* This is particularly true if the pain is of recent onset or has changed recently. Even if the client attributes the pain to heartburn or indigestion, this may be mistaken; it is not particularly uncommon for a patient who seeks medical advice complaining of indigestion to have serious heart disease. Conversely, it is important to be aware that clients with known, diagnosed heart disease are often very worried about the implications of their condition and may experience dyspnoea or chest pain as a result of their anxiety. Many such clients can benefit from acknowledgement and exploration of their fears and of the meanings which they attach to their illness.

Eysenck and his co-workers have claimed that a type of behaviour therapy termed *Creative Novation Therapy* is effective in reducing the risk of death from the most common type of heart disease, and also from cancer (Grossarth-Maticek and Eysenck, 1991; Eysenck and Grossarth-Maticek, 1991). However, the evidence for this claim has been convincingly challenged by others (Pelosi and Appleby, 1992). On the other hand, psycho-social interventions such as counselling do appear to relieve self-reported psychological distress in people suffering from heart disease and cancer (Hill et al., 1992).

**Palpitations and Dizzy Spells**

Unexpected conscious awareness of the beating of one's own heart is referred to as *palpitations*. Apart from some rare causes such as severe anaemia, palpitations are due either to heart disease or to anxiety. As discussed in the previous section, these two problems are not mutually exclusive. Heart disease causes palpitations when the heart beats irregularly, or unusually quickly or slowly. The palpitations of anxiety are typically experienced as rapid and regular, and are accompanied by other features of an anxiety state (see Table 4.3 in Chapter 4). *Clients who describe palpitations without other features of anxiety, in whom the symptom is new, or who are above the age of 35 years, should be referred for medical assessment.*

As well as causing palpitations, an abnormal rhythm to the heart beat may cause dizzy spells or even loss of consciousness. Dizzy spells can result from a variety of processes, biophysical or psychological, and the decision to refer must depend upon a number of factors including the severity and duration of the symptom and the presence or absence of associated symptoms. Obviously, *medical assessment is needed for a client whose dizzy spells sometimes result in loss of consciousness.* Such assessment will also be appropriate for a client with other signs or symptoms suggestive of biophysical disease. On the other hand, a client who gives a long history of dizzy spells along with other psychological symptoms is considerably less likely to have a medical cause.

*Clients who describe a rotational element to their dizziness should always be referred.* The subjective experience of rotation is known as *vertigo*, and may be described either as a sense of the environment moving round the person or of the person himself rotating in some direction. If severe, the vertigo may be accompanied by nausea or vomiting. Vertigo is almost always associated with biophysical disease of the ear, brain or other part of the nervous system (Cooper, 1993).

**Dyspepsia and Other Gastrointestinal Symptoms**

*Dyspepsia* is a rather vague term which refers to discomfort arising from the oesophagus (food pipe or gullet) or stomach. Together with the mouth and throat, these two organs constitute the upper part of the gastrointestinal tract which continues with the duodenum, small bowel and large bowel and terminates at the anus. Symptoms attributable to the gastrointestinal tract are so common as to be construed as normal much of the time. Most people, for example, would not regard themselves as ill if they were to experience a short-lived episode of mild heartburn, a few hours of nausea, occasional cramping pains in the abdomen or a temporary change in bowel habit. Most people would also recognise an association between gastrointestinal symptoms and their emotional state. Expressions such as 'sick with fear' and 'nervous hunger' are widely used and understood. It seems probable therefore that many clients will experience gastrointestinal symptoms whilst they are attending the counsellor and that some of these symptoms may be attributable to emotions associated with the counselling process. Much of the time, clients will either ignore these symptoms or accept them as emotional in origin.

Some people experience quite marked symptoms from their gastrointestinal tract which may be severe enough to affect their lives in some way but which are not associated with physical evidence of disease. The commonest of these symptoms are abdominal discomfort and abnormalities of bowel habit. This combination is described as the *irritable bowel syndrome*. Typically, the abdominal discomfort is relieved by defaecation and may be associated with changes in the frequency or consistency of the stool. The irritable bowel syndrome may also give rise to a feeling of bloating or abdominal distension, and to upper gastrointestinal symptoms such as nausea and vomiting. In addition, a few people with this syndrome describe symptoms related to the genito-urinary system such as frequent emptying of the bladder and a feeling of incomplete emptying after passing urine. Women may also describe pain on sexual intercourse. It is not clear whether the irritable bowel syndrome results from abnormalities of the normal pattern of contraction and relaxation of the bowel, abnormalities of sensation within the gastrointestinal tract, or abnormalities in the way these sensations are perceived and interpreted (Farthing, 1995). What is important from the counsellor's point of view is that the symptoms of irritable bowel syndrome are typically worse during periods of emotional stress and that patients with the syndrome are more likely to consult their doctor if they become depressed or anxious for some reason (Kettell et al., 1992). Although the symptoms can certainly be helped by dietary modification and prescribed drugs, attention to psychological and psychosocial issues can also bring great benefit (Friedman, 1991; Guthrie et al., 1993).

This section has discussed the so-called functional disorders of the gastrointestinal tract. These are conditions for which no underlying physical disease process can be identified. However, any of the symptoms described above may also result from potentially serious biophysical gastrointestinal disease. This is particularly likely in people above the age of 40 when the incidence of gastrointestinal cancer starts to increase. ***The counsellor should consider a medical referral for any client who describes a new gastrointestinal symptom.*** Another pointer towards the possibility of significant disease is the association of one or more gastrointestinal symptoms with recent loss of weight.

## Fatigue

Fatigue is a universal experience following a period of mental or physical exertion, or in the absence of needed sleep. However, some people experience fatigue at other times. Probably the commonest situation is in the context of emotional distress. Fatigue is a well recognised symptom of *depression*, for example (see the box entitled 'Major Depression', page 94, in Chapter 4). The client with clear features of a depressive illness and no other symptoms to suggest biophysical disease does not need medical investigation. However, a wide range of biophysical illnesses can also give rise to the symptom of fatigue (Ridsdale et al., 1993). Where this is of recent onset or without other psychological features, then the counsellor should consider referral.

A particular problem is that of the *chronic fatigue syndrome*, sometimes known as the *post-viral fatigue syndrome* or *myalgic encephalitis*. Fatigue during and for a few days or weeks after an episode of viral illness such as influenza or glandular fever is well known. However, in a small number of people the problem persists for months or years (Cope et al., 1994). Typically, the client complains of a tendency to fatigue quickly on exertion such that she is able to do far less than in the past. Furthermore, the sensation of fatigue following exertion may last for the rest of the day and may persist for another day or two beyond that. If the symptoms are severe, then the client may end up virtually bed-ridden, although most people with chronic fatigue syndrome remain mobile to some degree. Other symptoms typical of the syndrome include pain and tenderness of the muscles (worse after exercise), joint pains, headaches, frequent sore throats and a tendency 'to catch anything that is going', forgetfulness, irritability, difficulty in thinking, an inability to maintain previous levels of concentration and sleep disturbance (Holmes et al., 1988). Some people develop similar symptoms without an initial virus infection (Wessely et al., 1995). Although people with chronic fatigue syndrome may become depressed and exhibit typical features such as a low mood and ideas of hopelessness, the majority of people with the syndrome do not meet diagnostic criteria for depression and do not respond to anti-depressant medication. There is considerable uncertainty about the cause or causes of the syndrome and the various hypotheses are a matter of hot debate. The question of causality is of less practical relevance, however, than the issue of effective treatment. Most attempts to treat chronic fatigue syndrome appear to be no more effective than allowing nature to take its course (Ho-Yen, 1990; Lawrie and Pelosi, 1994). Recently, however, Sharpe et al. (1996) have described a form of cognitive-behavioural therapy that does appear to be effective in reducing symptoms and improving the day-to-day functioning of people with the syndrome. Other investigators are currently researching the effects of dietary supplements, and the potential benefits of graded exercise programmes in rehabilitation.

Biophysical disease processes such as an under-active thyroid gland, inflammation of the blood vessels or cancer of the blood cells can occasionally cause symptoms similar to those of chronic fatigue syndrome. *A client who appears to have the syndrome and who has not sought medical advice should be encouraged to do so,* although an alternative diagnosis is unlikely.

### Back Pain

Pain in the back or neck is an extremely common symptom, one that most people experience at some time in their lives (Humphrey, 1989). Probably the commonest variety is *chronic, non-specific low back pain* in which pain is felt across the lower back, in one or both buttocks and often down the back of one or both legs. The pain may persist for months or years and tends to cause more distress than disability. The precise cause is not clear in many cases. Some people with these symptoms may have a history of back injury or an abnormality of the spine that is visible on X-ray (Jayson, 1994), although it is not always clear that such factors are causally related to the pain.

Other varieties of low back pain are not uncommon. *Acute low back pain* may follow activity which the person is not used to, such as weight lifting. It may come on quite suddenly during an attempt to lift a heavy or awkward object with a bent back. The pain is often accompanied by a lot of spasm in the back muscles which may drastically limit mobility. Unless there is pre-existing chronic low back pain, acute back pain tends to get better completely within a few weeks. A related condition which may start quite abruptly is *sciatica*. This is due to pressure on the sciatic nerve which runs down the back of the leg, and commonly causes pain down the back of the leg all the way from the buttock to the heel. Sciatica is often accompanied by low back pain although the pain in the leg is usually the worse of the two. Sciatica usually improves with time although sometimes physiotherapy or an operation are needed to bring relief.

Long-standing back pain may follow an injury, either due to lifting as described above, or following a blow direct to the back. Much has been written in this context about '*compensation neurosis*'. It is said that some people with back pain following an injury do not improve until they have received adequate compensation from their employer or some other person whom they hold responsible. Although some people undoubtedly fake or exaggerate their symptoms ('*factitious symptoms*') the main mechanism of compensation neurosis is often said to be that of *secondary gain*. The idea is that although the pain is associated with discomfort and disability, it continues to be experienced and described to others because it brings benefits such as attention, and an expectation of monetary compensation.

Pain may be felt in the back other than in the lower spine. The second most common area is the neck. Neck pain may be long-standing or may come on unexpectedly and suddenly. A not uncommon problem is *acute torticollis*. Sufferers from this condition wake with a painful stiff neck which they can hardly bear to move so that the head is held tilted to one side, often with the face looking slightly upwards. This condition usually gets better in two or three days. Pain in the back of the chest or the middle of the back is less common and is more likely to be caused by a disease process requiring specific treatment.

There is a clear association between back pain and mood. A depressed client may admit to pain or discomfort in the back if asked directly, and many people with longstanding back problems find that the pain gets worse when they are anxious or depressed. Occasionally treatment directed at psychological illness may bring about dramatic improvement in the physical symptom of back pain.

The client with longstanding neck or back pain will probably accept this as part of his or her normal experience and may not mention it to the counsellor unless specifically asked. However, a new symptom or change in symptoms may lead to discussion with the counsellor. *Medical referral should always be considered even though the doctor may not ultimately be able to offer any kind of effective treatment beyond that of pain relief and advice on keeping active* (Waddell, 1993). The main purpose of medical assessment for most types of back pain is to exclude rare but treatable causes (Clinical Standards Advisory Group, 1994). *Referral should be particularly considered if the client is disabled in any way by the pain, exhibits signs such as a limp, is losing weight or has symptoms additional to pain in the back.*

## Hypertension

Systemic arterial hypertension, or *high blood pressure*, differs from the conditions discussed so far in that it rarely causes symptoms on its own. Hypertension matters because it increases the risk that a person will suffer a stroke or will develop disease of the heart or kidneys. Treatment can reduce a person's blood pressure and in doing so will reduce the risk that he or she will suffer a stroke. It may also prevent or delay the onset of heart or kidney disease. Hypertension is diagnosed when the blood pressure is sufficiently high that there is a significant risk of developing a stroke, heart disease or kidney disease, and when the potential benefits of treatment outweigh the potential risks. Because hypertension rarely causes symptoms, the condition is often diagnosed during a physical examination for another purpose, such as an insurance medical examination, or when a patient consults the doctor about an unrelated problem.

Treatment of high blood pressure is usually by medication, although the doctor may also advise regular exercise and a reduction in salt intake. An overweight patient may be advised to lose weight, and a heavy drinker to cut down, as these changes can also reduce the arterial blood pressure. The doctor should advise a smoker to stop. This will not reduce the patient's blood pressure, but smoking is another factor which increases the risk of having a stroke or developing heart disease.

Many of the drugs that are used to treat hypertension cause symptoms in some people, and a client may mention these to the counsellor. Symptoms induced by anti-hypertensive drugs include fatigue, headaches, weakness and impotence. Different anti-hypertensive drugs tend to cause different side effects so that a change in medication may help.

The diagnosis of hypertension can itself have adverse psycho-social effects, quite apart from any adverse effects of medication (Haynes et al., 1978). For some people the diagnosis may be the first time that they have had to face the possibility of illness in their lives and the inevitability of death. Other people have particular health beliefs concerning high blood pressure with which they may have difficulties in coming to terms. A relative, for example, may have suffered a disabling and distressing stroke. The diagnosis of hypertension is occasionally followed by marked anxiety or depression. As indicated at the beginning of this chapter, discussion of a client's health beliefs in relation to the diagnosis, and exploration of possible unconscious processes, may be very helpful in such circumstances.

## Chronic Illness, Disability and Pain

Some of the conditions already discussed in this chapter, such as angina, Parkinsonism, asthma and back pain, may result in chronic (long-term) ill-health and disability. Other frequent causes of chronic ill-health include lung damage from smoking or other causes, heart failure, arthritis, epilepsy (Scambler, 1989), stroke and multiple sclerosis (Robinson, 1988). A number of other chronic conditions, such as arterial hypertension and diabetes (Kelleher, 1988), are not in themselves causes of disability although their complications may be.

The experience of developing a chronic illness has been likened to that of finding an elephant in the living room. There may be no obvious reason why the elephant has turned up in this house rather than in the house next door. The presence of the elephant is most inconvenient, explanations must be offered to friends and relatives, and the whole household is affected by it. The elephant needs considerable care and attention, and alters the ways in which household members act and interact, but nobody has the power to make it go away.

Along with practical help such as welfare advice, nursing support, the provision of aids to living and the prescription of medication, people who develop a chronic disabling illness may need help in coming to terms with their changed circumstances. The same may also be true for their close family members. The role of the counsellor may be to help his client address the question 'Why me?' and to deal with a sense of injustice, and with feelings of anger or shame. The client may resent the apparent good health of others (including the counsellor), may grieve for what he has lost, and may be anxious about the future. The reader will note close parallels between the emotional response to chronic illness and the emotional response to bereavement.

A particularly distressing component of some chronic conditions is *chronic pain*. The management of pain has three components: biophysical, psychological and behavioural. Biophysical treatments include pain killers and other medication, physiotherapy, surgical interventions, acupuncture and so forth. Many people who suffer chronic pain are also helped by various psychological interventions. This is especially likely to be true if they are depressed or anxious; reduction in emotional distress is often accompanied by a reduction in the reported severity of pain. Finally, behavioural measures can be very helpful in the context of chronic pain. Advice to take appropriate exercise has long been given by doctors, physiotherapists and others. Although the rationale has often been biophysical (to mobilise stiff, painful joints, for example), the benefits may also be psychosocial (increasing the patient's sense of control over his body, and promoting social interaction). More recently, interventions have been developed with an explicit theoretical basis in behavioural psychology (France and Robson, 1986).

## HIV and AIDS

*Human immunodeficiency virus (HIV)* is an important contemporary cause of chronic illness and disability. It is transmitted via infected body fluids, typically through sexual intercourse, sharing of needles by injecting drug users, or through accidental needle-stick injury. Occasionally the virus may be transmitted in other ways, through use of non-sterile tattooing needles, for example. In the past, many people became infected through transfusion with infected blood or blood products.

When a person is first infected with the virus he or she may suffer HIV seroconversion illness. This typically lasts from one to two weeks, with a fever, muscular pains and sometimes night sweats. Other common features are joint pains and a skin rash. The person may describe loss of energy and feeling unwell, sometimes persisting for months after other symptoms and signs of the illness have disappeared. Other persisting symptoms may be headache and depressed mood. It is important to note that the usual tests for HIV infection may be negative during the seroconversion illness. They normally become positive within six weeks of infection, but may take up to three months.

Following the seroconversion illness, most people with HIV infection return to apparently normal health. This may last for five or more years, although appropriate blood tests will always show the continuing presence of HIV infection. During this time the person's resistance to a range of other infections, such as tuberculosis, pneumonia and candida (thrush), is gradually weakening. In addition, they will become increasingly susceptible to a range of other diseases such as various kinds of cancer, and dementia (see below). Sooner or later, unless they die of some unrelated cause beforehand, all people with HIV will develop a disease or diseases that are directly attributable to the effects of infection with the virus. Acquired immune deficiency syndrome (AIDS) is the label used to describe the diagnosis in a person with HIV infection of one or more infections or other diseases that are uncommon in people without HIV but relatively common in people nearing the end of their life with HIV. Thus at any one time, most people with HIV infection are not suffering from AIDS, although most will eventually develop AIDS. Some, however, will die of unrelated causes, while others will die of HIV-related conditions without developing AIDS. Partly for this reason, there is an increasing tendency to talk about HIV infection and HIV-related disease rather than use the more limited term AIDS.

Many diseases lead ultimately to chronic illness and death. However, particular issues arise in relation to counselling people with HIV infection. A person infected with the virus may know others who are also infected, and may have lost friends or partners as a result of HIV-related diseases. They may therefore have particular expectations of the likely course of their illness – expectations which may or may not prove valid – and their emotional response to their own illness may influence, and be influenced by, their emotional responses to the HIV-related illnesses of others.

People living with HIV infection may contemplate suicide. Suicidal behaviour is especially likely following initial diagnosis, and in the later stages of the illness as symptoms and disability become more severe. Other factors which may make suicide or attempted suicide more likely include depressed mood, other psychosocial problems, alcohol or substance abuse, and poor social support. In the period immediately following diagnosis, adequate pre- and post-HIV test counselling are likely to be important in reducing the risk of suicide. Such counselling is normally the responsibility of the doctor who arranges the test. Pre-test counselling should address the following issues:

- assessment of the person's risk of being infected;
- provision of information about the HIV virus, how it is trans-mitted, its effects and its medical management;
- explanation and discussion of the social and legal implications of undertaking the test, and of a positive result;
- assessment of the person's potential reaction to a positive test result, their coping mechanisms and social support; and
- discussion of issues of confidentiality.

If the test result is negative then the doctor should discuss strategies for prevention, and should consider with the patient whether a further test is needed in three months' time. If the result is positive then the doctor should state this clearly, and allow the patient sufficient time to discuss their emotional reaction and immediate concerns. The doctor should clarify any misconcep-tions and may need to offer a further explanation of the disease and its implications. The doctor should also discuss ways of avoiding infecting others, re-assess the patient's social support, and enquire after the patient's immediate plans for coping.

The diagnosis of HIV infection immediately raises the question of how it occurred, and this may have significant implications for a person's family, social and work relationships. People with HIV, regardless of how they were infected, all suffer from what has been termed 'co-categorisation' – the prejudicial assumption that they must have been infected through deviant or illicit acts. The issue of confidentiality is therefore of special significance. In medical practices and other medical settings, records are often freely accessible to all members of the team. Such a policy may not always be appropriate, and some of the issues for the counsellor are discussed in Chapter 5. The person to whom a disclosure is made owes a duty of confidentiality to their patient or client in respect of that disclosure. If the disclosure is of a sensitive matter such as infection with the HIV virus, then unless consent is given to pass the information on to others, it is prudent to keep it to oneself. An important exception is if the client is behaving or intends to behave in a manner that will put others at significant risk. An often quoted example is where, despite clearly stated advice and discussion, a married man with HIV does not inform his wife but demonstrates a clear intention of continuing to have unprotected sexual intercourse with her. In such circumstances the counsellor should consider informing the wife and may be liable in law if she does not do so. It would be important to make a very full record of all that was said between the client and the counsellor, and it would also be wise for the counsellor to discuss the problem with her supervisor and to seek legal advice before taking any action that would breach confidentiality.

One of the effects of the HIV virus, usually occurring late in the disease process, is *AIDS dementia*. Dementia generally refers to global loss of mental function, especially intellectual and other cognitive abilities. In AIDS dementia, sometimes called AIDS dementia complex (ADC), the first symptom is often difficulty in concentrating. Forgetfulness is also common, and some people become aware that their thinking is slowed down. Later symptoms are clumsiness, sloppy handwriting, tremor and poor balance. The symptoms generally develop over a period of weeks or months. AIDS dementia may improve with appropriate medication, so a client with HIV who describes the early symptoms should be referred for medical assessment.

## Diet and Health

We all need food to live and an appropriate diet to stay healthy. Indeed, Maslow (1943) pointed out many years ago that until basic physiological needs such as food and drink are met, a person's needs for safety, love, esteem and self-actualization are likely to take second place. In order to maintain long-term health, a person's diet requires adequate and appropriate amounts of energy (calories), protein, fibre, fats, minerals, vitamins and water. This implies a mixed intake of different foodstuffs such that over the course of any few days all these basic requirements are covered.

Diet, physical health and psychosocial well-being can affect one another in a number of ways. Both physical illness and emotional distress may be associated with changes in appetite, and hence in the quantity and variety of food intake. On the other hand, too much or too little of any of the basic dietary requirements may impair physical or psychological health. For example, a grossly inadequate intake of vitamin B1 (thiamine) may cause tiredness, irritability, poor memory, poor appetite, abdominal discomfort and constipation. If the deficiency is not corrected, then pain and weakness may develop in the legs, or confusion and severe impairment of short-term memory (*Korsakoff syndrome*). Other possible effects are loss of co-ordination, heart failure and eventually death. These problems are most often seen in people whose diet consists of little other than polished rice, but can also occur in long-term, heavy drinkers. Another example of ill-health due to inadequate intake of a vitamin is *scurvy*. This is due to vitamin C deficiency and causes weakness, aches and pains, swollen, bleeding gums and bruising in the skin. Heavy drinkers occasionally develop scurvy, and so do others whose diet lacks sources of vitamin C such as fresh fruit and vegetables.

Dietary deficiencies of vitamins and of most minerals are, however, rare in the developed world. It is unwise to attribute symptoms to such deficiency without good reason. If you do suspect such deficiency then you should refer the client for medical assessment. Supplementing the diet with vitamins or minerals without evidence of deficiency can be dangerous; too high an intake of certain vitamins (including vitamins A, B6, D, E and K) and of certain minerals (such as iron) may cause serious harm. An excellent summary of the clinical effects of dietary deficiencies and excesses is provided by Berkow and Fletcher (1992).

Another way in which diet may influence health is through the effects of food additives. There is little or no good evidence that approved additives are harmful to the majority of people.

However, some people do suffer adverse reactions to certain additives. Such reactions may include asthma, skin rashes or migraine. Disorders of eating behaviour, including *anorexia nervosa* and *bulimia*, are discussed in Chapter 4.

## Premenstrual Syndrome, Pregnancy, Childbirth and the Menopause

The final section of this chapter is concerned with a number of life experiences which are particular to women, and which may raise issues for both counsellors and their medical colleagues.

### Premenstrual Syndrome

The notion of a premenstrual syndrome dates back at least 60 years (Frank, 1931). The term is widely used to describe physical, psychological and even behavioural symptoms that are experienced during the period between ovulation and menstruation. The possible symptoms include weight gain, painful breasts, swelling of the abdomen, swollen hands and feet, headache, back ache, general aches and pains, difficulty concentrating, lethargy and irritability (Richardson, 1989).

The cause or causes of the premenstrual syndrome are unclear. Several theories relate to changing levels of hormones that circulate in the blood, or changes in certain chemicals in the brain. These theories have given rise to attempts to 'treat' the premenstrual syndrome with medication such as pyridoxine (vitamin B6) (Doll et al., 1989). Although some women do report some benefit from such treatments, they rarely find that all their premenstrual symptoms are relieved. This is not surprising, as there is every reason to believe that there is more to the premenstrual syndrome than changes in hormones and other chemicals. Indeed, some writers have suggested that the social construction of a premenstrual syndrome owes much to a dominant androcentric perspective within western culture (Nicolson, 1992).

On the other hand, Ussher (1992) has suggested that women do tend to experience physical and other changes about themselves prior to menstruation, but that the ways in which they experience these changes, the labels that they give them and the causes to which they attribute them are culturally influenced. A pragmatic approach for the counsellor may be to acknowledge the reality of premenstrual symptoms described by a client and to respect her right to seek medical advice if she wishes, while not actively encouraging her to do so (see also pages 78–9).

### Pregnancy and Childbirth

Much has been written about the implications of pregnancy and childbirth for the mental health and emotional well-being of women and their families (Hunter, 1994; Walker, 1990). These are times of great change, and many pregnant women and their partners will admit to periods of anxiety associated with fantasies about problems with the baby or negative consequences of the pregnancy.

An issue that may arise early in pregnancy is that of termination. This is an option which passes through the minds of many women who may wish to discuss it and to air their feelings in order to make a decision. In Britain at the time of writing termination of pregnancy is legal under the Abortion Act 1967 and subsequent amendments, if two registered medical practitioners certify the need for termination under one or more of the following circumstances:

■ that continuance of the pregnancy would involve risk to the life of the pregnant woman greater than if the pregnancy were terminated;
■ that termination is necessary to prevent grave permanent injury to the physical or mental health of the pregnant woman;
■ that there is a substantial risk that if the child were born it would suffer from such physical or mental abnormalities as to be seriously handicapped;
■ that the pregnancy has not exceeded its 24th week and that the continuance of the pregnancy would involve risk, greater than if the pregnancy were terminated, of injury to the physical or mental health of the pregnant woman; or
■ that the pregnancy has not exceeded its 24th week and that the continuance of the pregnancy would involve risk, greater than if the pregnancy were terminated, of injury to the physical or mental health of any existing children of the family of the pregnant woman.

There is no time limit on the first three conditions; termination under any of these is legal up to term. However, terminations after about 13 weeks' gestation become progressively more difficult to undertake, and many gynaecologists will refuse to terminate a pregnancy after about 16 weeks. A woman who decides to seek a termination will find it easier to arrange and will suffer less physical trauma the earlier she does so.

A woman who has undergone termination of pregnancy may experience feelings of guilt and remorse weeks, months or years later. A potent trigger that may bring such feelings to the fore is subsequent difficulty in conceiving a wanted child. A woman's knowledge that the decision to undergo termination was ultimately her own may compound her feelings of guilt and make it doubly difficult for her to disclose these feelings. This is an area where the counsellor's own values, beliefs, previous decisions and personal experiences may significantly affect his or her ability to respond helpfully and appropriately to the client, and highlights the importance of adequate training and ongoing supervision.

For those women who continue with a pregnancy, the time following delivery often brings significant emotional problems. '*Baby blues*' are well known, and refer to the depressed affect and feelings of misery that are very common during the first few days. *Post-natal depression* (see also page 79) is far more serious and affects between 5 and 22 per cent of women during the first twelve months following delivery (Richards, 1990). Many women with a history of recurrent depression become depressed during the first post-natal year but others experience their first episode during this time. Two factors in particular appear to make a woman vulnerable to post-natal depression. These are a poor relationship between herself and her partner, and poor quality social support with a lack of availability of a confidant.

Sadly, not all pregnancies end with the delivery of a healthy baby. Miscarriages, still-births, pre-term deliveries and abnormalities of the newborn baby all occur. Any of these outcomes may have a devastating effect on the emotional state of the woman and her partner, and on their processes of family interaction. A very common feeling following an adverse outcome of pregnancy is that of guilt, often accompanied by recriminations against the self or others.

Even when the eventual outcome of the pregnancy has been a healthy child, some women feel resentment or other negative emotions as a result of their experiences during labour. The woman who has planned a home birth but ends up in hospital having her baby delivered by forceps may subsequently feel angry at herself and at others. Two factors which appear important in reducing a woman's dissatisfaction with her treatment during labour and childbirth are continuity of care by a single midwife, and the opportunity to retain a sense of control over what is done to her.

## Menopause

Strictly speaking, the menopause refers to a woman's last menstrual period and can thus be recognised only in retrospect. By convention, unless a woman is pregnant, or has some other reason that stops her from menstruating, then cessation of all periods for six months is taken as indicating that the last period was the menopause. *Any bleeding after this time is regarded as post-menopausal bleeding and requires medical investigation.*

The menopause usually occurs between the ages of 45 and 55 years, although some women experience this event earlier in their lives. The period of time preceding and following the menopause is known as the perimenopause or climacteric, and many women experience a number of symptoms during this time. Their periods may become heavy or irregular in both frequency and flow before the menopause. Although these changes are rarely the result of disease, they do require medical assessment. Many women experience hot flushes and night sweats. The flushes usually last a few minutes, although they can be longer, and the woman has an unpleasant sensation of heat spreading over the face, neck and chest. This sensation may be accompanied by sweating, can occur at any time of the day or night, and may occur anything between once every few days and many times a day.

Other physical symptoms that are common at the time of the menopause or afterwards are thinning of the skin and bodily hair, loss of shape and reduction in firmness of the breasts, and aches and pains in the joints (Dickson and Henriques, 1992). Later on, the lining of the vagina can become thin and dry. This may lead to discomfort or pain during and after sexual intercourse. Some women also experience impairment of bladder control with sudden urges to pass water or some degree of urinary incontinence. Most of these physical symptoms tend to improve if the woman takes hormone replacement therapy.

In addition to physical changes, emotional difficulties are common at the menopause. These may include irritability, difficulty in concentrating, sleep disturbance and feelings of tiredness. Frank clinical depression may develop, and this may be a first episode or a recurrence of previous depressive illness. Although in the past such psychological problems have been attributed by some to the hormonal changes that occur during the perimenopause, hormone replacement therapy alone rarely brings much relief. It seems likely that a number of environmental and social factors are far more important in many cases. These may include children leaving home, dissatisfaction with social or work circumstances and, perhaps most important of all, unresolved difficulties in the woman's marriage or other long-term relationship. Loss of fertility, deterioration in health and awareness of ageing may also play an important part in the distress of some women at this time.

Couples may become less sexually active at or after the menopause. Physical changes and emotional processes both play a part, while reduced sexual activity may bring to the fore other problems within a relationship. On the other hand, some couples enjoy sex more as the possibility of pregnancy recedes. Unless the woman or her partner is sterile then conception may occur up to two years following the menopause before the age of 50, or up to one year post-menopause after this age.

Apart from menstrual irregularities, physical menopausal symptoms do not of themselves require medical assessment unless the woman feels that drug or other treatment would be useful. The value of hormone replacement therapy at the time of the menopause and afterwards in reducing the complications of osteoporosis in later life is now well established. Hormone replacement also appears to reduce the risk of heart attacks and strokes, and to protect against cancer of the womb and ovaries. Although radically challenged by some commentators (Greer, 1991), current medical opinion is that long-term hormone replacement therapy should be offered to any woman at about the time of the menopause who does not have a clear reason for not using it.

## Conclusion

In this chapter we have discussed a number of common symptoms and other problems which clients may describe during counselling. Such disclosures raise a number of issues for the counsellor. Is there an underlying biophysical disease, significant psychosocial process, or both? Why has the client disclosed this problem, in this way, at this time? What might be the implications of the problem for the counselling process, and of counselling for the client's illness? How is the client coping with the problem, and what are the implications of his or her coping behaviour? We have not attempted the impossible task of being comprehensive in addressing these questions, but have tried in this chapter and elsewhere in the book to describe common scenarios, to highlight significant issues, and to illustrate important principles.

An immediate question that the counsellor may face is that of whether or not to advise the client to seek medical advice for a newly disclosed symptom. ***Clients should never be dissuaded from obtaining medical assessment for any problem once they have decided to seek it, and the counsellor should always consider recommending such assessment for new symptoms, or if a client reports a long-standing symptom as becoming more severe, or as changing in some way.*** If the counsellor does not already work in a medical setting such as a general practice, then she should consider developing a relationship with a local general practitioner or other doctor with whom she can discuss medical issues while keeping her clients' identity confidential.

# 4

## Psychiatric Conditions and their Treatment in Relation to Counselling

### What is Meant by Mental Illness?

Psychiatry is a branch of medicine which deals with the symptoms and signs related to aspects of thought, perception, emotion, behaviour, intellect or personality rather than bodily functions, such as gastrointestinal functioning or respiratory functioning. As we shall see, the dividing line between psychiatric and physical disorders is not clear cut, as the presenting symptoms of many physical disorders can be psychological and vice versa.

Differences between mental health and illness, and what is considered normal and abnormal in psychological terms, are perhaps not so easily determined as in physical medicine. However, there are some concepts which are useful. Generally, in medicine, the concept of a *syndrome* is applied to a collection of symptoms which can be recognised as commonly occurring together in an identifiable pattern. When it is possible further to define an underlying biophysical process that can be demonstrated to cause this syndrome, the term *disease* is used. For most syndromes in physical medicine the term 'disease' can be applied. This is not so in psychiatry, but increasingly it is possible to identify that biophysical processes in the brain play a part in the development of schizophrenia and severe depression. The physical cause of dementia, in terms of changes in the brain and nervous system, has been known for a very long time.

So when does a psychiatrist use the term *mental illness?* Generally when a clear syndrome can be identified, there has been a definite change from how the person used to be and there is a deterioration in the person's ability to function effectively. This is important in differentiating illness from 'personality disorder' which is not viewed as 'illness'. Dependence on alcohol or drugs is similarly not viewed as being mental illness, but again psychiatrists are often involved in treatment in order to attempt to relieve suffering either as experienced by the person themselves or those around them. We shall use the generic term *serious mental health problems* to encompass serious mental illness, addictions and personality disorder. By serious mental illness we mean the presence of considerable loss of ability to function normally, and/or considerable suffering, often with the addition of delusions or hallucinations (defined below). We recognise that some counsellors, particularly those with a humanistic orientation, will be reluctant to consider the use of 'diagnoses'. A diagnosis is useful only if it can be helpful in predicting the use of an effective treatment. Personality disorder is a lifelong abnormality of personality. Psychiatrists have spent many years inventing categorical labels for abnormal personalities but people rarely fit one exactly. Use of these labels should be exercised with some caution as labels tend to be very sticky and the presence of a personality disorder does not preclude the additional development of mental illness. A typology of the more commonly used terms can be found in Appendix 8, page 134. In practice most people, normal or abnormal, possess a number of different traits rather than easily fitting into one category. Some people may appear to have personality difficulties but these are in fact only apparent when they have a mental illness. Exploration of their past may not reveal any previous indication of personality problem and in this case the term *personality disorder* is not applicable and may in fact be detrimental to the patient.

*David works in an agency which has a consultant psychiatrist attached to it. David refers Fred, the client, to the psychiatrist for an assessment and report. The report on Fred is descriptive, simply says that Fred is not mentally ill, and makes no treatment recommendations. David is convinced that Fred is quite disturbed but well motivated and David wants to help. In the case of this professional disagreement, what can or should David do?*

Comment: *A person can be significantly psychologically disturbed without having a formally diagnosable 'mental illness'. A common criticism of psychiatrists (frequently justified) is that they often limit their reports to an opinion about the presence or absence of 'mental illness' and then do not give any recommendations for what to do in the absence of this. The psychiatrist may consider that Fred has personality problems which may not be helped, or may possibly be exacerbated, by counselling if it is deeper than the supportive level. In the first instance David should discuss the problem with the psychiatrist and ask for further clarification. If this is not forthcoming, the next step depends on the view of the organisation in which David works. The matter should be raised with them. If this route is not satisfactory, David should encourage Fred to consult his GP and offer to discuss the matter with a view to obtaining a second opinion.*

This example also raises the issues of how psychiatrists perceive counsellors and how the counsellor should set about communicating with the GP or mental health professionals. We will return to these matters below.

A further complicating factor is that judgements about appropriateness of behaviour and beliefs are often made without due attention being paid to cultural context. Concern has been expressed about the tendency for more people from Afro-Caribbean culture to receive the diagnosis of schizophrenia in the United Kingdom when compared with people from other cultures. There is also evidence that people from Asian cultures tend to express depression more frequently in terms of physical symptoms than those from European cultures. These issues, however, remain controversial and are well explored from mainstream and more radical viewpoints in Rack (1982) and Fernando (1988), respectively.

This discussion may seem laboured, but the presence of defined mental illness has significance in law, both in considering an individual's responsibility for his or her actions and when compulsory detention or treatment is being considered under the Mental Health Act (in order to identify the various 'sections' of the Act, see Appendix 7, page 132, for an introduction, Kendell

(1975) and Clare (1988) for further discussion of the concept of 'illness').

## Models in Psychiatry

People often assume that psychiatrists employ only the biological model. This model seeks physical causes in order to confirm the presence of 'disease', carrying out physical investigations like the new developments in brain imaging, such as CAT scanning (Computerised Axial Tomography: a way of taking pictures of slices through the brain with X-rays), which have undoubtedly brought about a revolution in the understanding of how the brain functions; and of course prescribing drugs and electro-convulsive therapy. The *biological* model is undoubtedly important, and this perspective is often that which a medically trained individual can exclusively provide. However, the *psychological* and *social* perspectives, which can be provided by a range of non-medically trained professionals, are seen as being of equal importance in psychiatry (see Anthony Clare's excellent book *Psychiatry in Dissent* (Clare, 1988)), in terms of fully understanding the causes of a person's problems, what investigations to carry out and what treatment is required. Counselling and psychotherapeutic approaches can be employed in conjunction with drug treatments and practical social help; for example, with housing problems. Counselling is never contra-indicated in someone with serious mental illness; what must be considered is the appropriate level of work. We will return to this later.

In understanding an individual and his or her problems, no single model can provide all the answers, so an experienced psychiatrist learns the value of eclecticism, and the importance of working as part of a team both within the secondary care setting (psychologist, social worker, occupational therapist, community psychiatric nurse) and in primary care (GP, health visitor, practice nurse, counsellor, physiotherapist) to make the best of the varied knowledge and skills each member has to offer.

## How Common is Mental Illness in the Community?

Depending on which set of criteria are used in research, around 4–13 per cent of the population have mental illness at any one time. However, there is now more or less international agreement on, for example, what constitutes *depression* or *schizophrenia*. In the course of a year, 12 million adults attending GP surgeries have psychiatric symptoms (mostly of anxiety and/or depression). Only 1 in 10 of those so recognised by the GP is referred to a psychiatrist, and only 1 in 1000 are severely enough depressed to require admission to hospital. About 40 per cent of those with depression are not recognised by the GP, largely because they also have physical illness, which the doctor focuses on exclusively, or they present with somatic symptoms of emotional distress. For reasons that are still not entirely clear, more women than men receive a diagnosis of mental illness, although men are selectively more likely to be referred to secondary care services (Mental Health Foundation, 1990).

## Who (Apart from Counsellors) are Involved in Assessing and Treating Mental Health Problems?

*Psychiatrists* are medically qualified and undergo a further minimum of six years' postgraduate training prior to appointment as a consultant in the National Health Service. However, doctors training in psychiatry (also referred to as 'psychiatrists') may have a varying level of experience. Some psychiatrists work in association with Community Mental Health Teams (CMHTs) and some also work in close liaison with GPs in primary care settings. Although all members of the Royal College of Psychiatrists (essential for consultant status) are expected to have received some training and supervision in psychotherapy, few have achieved a high level of expertise either in psychodynamic or behavioural therapies. This tends to be the case only for those who are appointed as consultant psychotherapists. Referral is generally only possible via the person's GP or another doctor. Many NHS consultants also have sessions in private practice.

*Psychotherapists* may come from a range of backgrounds. Those employed within the health service can be psychiatrists who have undergone further training in psychotherapy, or they may come from one of the other professions allied to medicine. Many psychotherapists also work in private practice and for non-statutory organisations concerned with the care of people with mental health problems (such as the Philadelphia Association, the Arbours Association). All psychotherapists working within both the public and private sectors can now apply for UKCP registration, which guarantees that they have achieved a degree of training approved by the United Kingdom Council for Psychotherapy.

*Community psychiatric nurses (CPNs)* are qualified Registered Mental Nurses who work outside the hospital setting often as members of a CMHT. Some also have close liaison with primary care. Although specific training for work in community settings does exist in the form of diploma courses, not all CPNs have undergone this. CPNs usually have not received any training in counselling or psychotherapy during their training, although GPs often assume they are qualified to 'counsel'. Direct referral to CPNs from primary care or other agencies is often (but not always) possible.

*Behavioural nurse specialists* are psychiatric nurses who have completed specialised training in behavioural therapy. Sometimes they work alongside clinical psychologists or independently take referrals directly from GPs. They do not necessarily have experience of community psychiatric nursing.

*Social workers (SWs)* The majority of social workers in the mental health field have the CQSW (Certificate of Qualification in Social Work) and work as part of a CMHT, a Local Authority Area Social Services Team or in other specialist areas such as Child Guidance Clinics, Community Alcohol Teams and so on. Social workers with specific training and experience in mental health problems who have special powers under the Mental Health Act (see Appendix 7, page 132), are known as *Approved Social Workers (ASWs)*. Most social workers have training in basic counselling skills and a minority have specific psychotherapeutic training often in fields such as family or marital therapy. A small number of SWs (fewer than in the past) have close links with GPs. Social workers take referrals from a range of agencies and individuals.

*Clinical psychologists* have a degree in Psychology and a postgraduate qualification in Clinical Psychology. As part of their course all will have learned about all aspects of psychological assessment and treatment, but their specific expertise will depend on their experience and therapeutic orientation (such as behavioural, cognitive, neuropsychological, psychodynamic). Some are members of CMHTs and some liaise closely with GPs. Direct referral is generally possible without first referring to the psychiatric service.

*Occupational therapists* work throughout the health service in a range of settings. Those who work in mental health are based in a hospital setting or in the community, often in a CMHT, and have training and experience in group skills and usually also counselling skills. Referral is via the psychiatric service. Some have undergone specific training in counselling or psychotherapy.

*Community Mental Health Teams* In many areas, mental health professionals in the community work as a team and all referrals in that area are made not to individual professionals, but to the 'Team', who then decide on who has the most appropriate skills to take the assessment forward. The majority of teams have a psychiatrist as a member, but the input of psychology is variable and the re-organisation of community care has tended to threaten the provision of social workers to such teams. Teams vary in taking referrals only from GPs or from a broader range of agencies in the community. Some accept self-referrals.

*General Practitioners* In order to be a Principal in general practice it is now necessary to have undergone vocational training (three years' post-registration, one of which is as a trainee in a general practice). Experienced, older GPs often have not undergone this training, and of those who are vocationally trained only 40 per cent have any specific experience in psychiatry beyond what they learned at medical school. GPs have a variable knowledge of counselling, although younger doctors will have received communication skills training at medical school and as a trainee, often employing the use of video, role-play or actors. It has been demonstrated that, although there has been a growth in the number of people employed as counsellors within general practice, a significant minority of GPs do not sufficiently understand what they do, for whom counselling would be appropriate, or what their qualifications are (Sibbald et al., 1993).

*Practice nurses* are Registered General Nurses who are employed directly by GP practices and have a variety of experience. Although some are expected to provide 'counselling', few have adequate training or supervision.

*Health Visitors* are Registered General Nurses with a further qualification in health visiting. They play a key role in the recognition of post-natal depression, and some have received specific training in counselling to help them in managing this particularly common form of depression.

## Communicating with Other Professionals (and the Client)

Good communication is crucial to the provision of quality mental health care. However, in practice all the professionals involved may treat one another with some suspicion and view counsellors as impinging on their territory. It will be easier for the counsellor to relate to the primary care team if he or she works in such a setting, but this may be more difficult if they work elsewhere. Whether or not such communication actually takes place will depend on the nature of the therapeutic contract with the client, the setting and the nature of the problem posed by the client's mental state. (Some of these issues are discussed further in Chapters 1 (assessment) and 5 (ethical issues of communicating with other professionals.) Where the counsellor works outside the primary care setting, he or she may in most cases simply advise the client to seek further help from the GP.

In any communication with another professional it is important for the counsellor to describe succinctly the problem they are concerned about, how the client came into their care, the terms of their therapeutic contract including aims and goals, and what they would like the GP or psychiatrist to address. It is also crucially important to say exactly what they have said to the client. In many of the sections of this chapter referral is advised. We do not apologise for this. Mental health problems require skilled assessment and treatment and clients deserve the best possible care. They also deserve an adequate explanation for why the counsellor feels that it necessary to ask for someone else to see them. A positive rather than negative reason for involving someone else is essential and negotiation must be carried out sensitively, while recognising that in some cases clear advice may be needed. Not 'I can't cope with you' but rather 'this puzzles me . . . I think it would help both of us if I asked someone else to see you . . . what do you think?'

Mental health workers vary in their attitudes towards counselling. Some feel that counsellors may miss physically based mental disorders in clients who present to them (see, for example, Persaud, 1993). Others recognise that many people do not want or need to have their problems 'medicalised' and that there is no realistic need for competition given the level of need for skilled psychological help in the community. There is, however, a realistic concern that all counsellors should be able to recognise when they have reached the limits of their training and expertise in helping someone with more complex problems.

## Recognising and Responding to Serious Mental Health Problems

Most textbooks approach this topic from the viewpoint of diagnosis rather than presenting problems. We have opted for the alternative viewpoint. For detailed descriptions see the official guides such as *The ICD-10 Classification of Mental and Behavioural Diseases* (WHO, 1993) or the *American Psychiatric Association Diagnostic and Statistical Manual DSM-IV* (APA, 1994), used widely in research, or a textbook of psychopathology such as Pfeffer and Waldron (1987), from which the framework below has been adapted.

We have indicated when medical involvement would be preferable but is not essential, when an assessment must be sought from the GP and when we feel that the Mental Health Services really should be involved either through the GP or directly. The route taken will depend on the setting in which the counsellor is working (if attached to primary care liaison with the GP should be easier), the client preference and the accessibility of the mental health service to referral other than through the GP.

## Appearance

### Changes in Appearance
*These may be due to underlying physical problems*: for example, after mutilating surgery, or due to hormonal problems or medication. These problems will usually be apparent on referral, and difficulty in coming to terms with changed appearance may be part of the reason for the referral.

*They may be self-induced*: repetitive self-mutilation is a common feature of some people with severe personality problems. Very occasionally some people who damage their skin do not admit that this is self-induced but seek treatment for this (*Dermatitis artefacta*).

### Dissatisfaction with Appearance

This is known as *Dysmorphophobia*. Transient feelings of un-happiness with one's appearance are common in adolescence and may also reflect a sensitive, insecure personality. Some people are undoubtedly helped by plastic surgery, but most surgeons have close links with interested psychologists and psychiatrists who carry out assessments before the operation takes place. Rarely, however, people become totally preoccupied, sometimes in a very bizarre way, such that they lose touch with reality and become deluded. They may be driven to self-mutilation. When present to this severe extent, this indicates serious mental illness, possibly schizophrenia, and urgent psychiatric assessment is essential.

### Lack of Care for One's Appearance

Sudden deterioration of self-care can occur in a number of different illnesses, most commonly depression, but also schizo-phrenia and organic brain diseases such as dementia. A person with mania (described further below) sometimes adopts an uncharacteristically bright appearance or a style of dress which is unusual for them. This can be difficult to judge at first meeting but is clearly apparent when a longer relationship enables comparison with previous appearance or dress.

### Unusual Movements

Many odd movements are associated with serious mental illness, but it is not appropriate to mention the majority of them here as they tend to be very rare and most occur in chronic schizophrenic illnesses for which the person is unlikely to be receiving coun-selling. Movement disorders are discussed in detail from a physical perspective elsewhere (see pages 42–4). A common problem which causes concern is *tremor*. This can be commonly due to anxiety, but it can also be caused by withdrawal from alcohol and too much caffeine. Some movements can be associated with medication. *Drug-induced movements* are discussed in detail later.

Lack of movement can be an important indicator of severe psychiatric illness. In its severest form this is called *stupor* and **urgent psychiatric referral is essential**. There is an absence of speech and movement but the person remains completely conscious. Often there is a failure to eat and drink, and this is one of the rare instances when ECT is used and can be life-saving. In much lesser forms depression can lead to *psychomotor retardation*, which means being slowed down in both thought and action. The retarded person looks depressed and generally delays before answering questions. They often appear much less slowed up if seen in the evening rather than the morning. Retardation is known as a *biological* symptom of depression and such symptoms generally respond well to drug treatment. If there is clear evidence of retardation, the GP should be involved and referral possibly then made to the mental health services (depending on severity), as anti-depressant treatment must be considered.

## Eating Problems

### Loss of Appetite and/or Weight
This is commonly a symptom of depression. In severe depression weight loss can be marked and rapid and there may be other biological symptoms (sleep disturbance, loss of energy, retardation). Some patients who become psychotically depressed may even have the delusion that they cannot eat because their bowels have rotted away. People with other forms of psychiatric illness can lose weight. In mania people lose weight because their numerous plans and increasingly busy life leave them little time to eat. In schizophrenia, weight can be lost because of paranoid delusions that food is poisoned. In dementia people may forget to buy and prepare food.

### Anorexia Nervosa
In younger people who are losing weight it is important to consider anorexia nervosa. A great deal has been written elsewhere about this condition – for example, Crisp (1990) for a psychiatrist's view; McLeod (1981) for the sufferer's view – so we shall not dwell on it in detail here. This is primarily a condition of adolescent or young women, but 10–15 per cent of cases do occur in young males. The weight loss is usually associated with a 'morbid fear of fatness' and loss of menstrual periods. There may also be bingeing and vomiting, abuse of laxatives or diuretics and excessive exercising and clear physical signs of malnutrition. If

there is clear evidence of marked loss of weight psychiatric referral should be sought, although this will need to be carefully negotiated with the client. ***When weight loss is severe urgent psychiatric assessment must be obtained***, as in such cases hospitalisation might be needed as a life-saving measure.

### Increased Appetite and/or Weight

Overeating may be associated with depression. Some people who are depressed are prone to 'comfort eating'. Binge eating occurs in bulimia nervosa. In this group, weight is generally maintained within normal limits and bingeing is followed by self-induced vomiting. It occurs almost exclusively in women. Bingeing differs from 'normal' overeating because it is experienced as being 'out of control'. Many people are very secretive about their bingeing and vomiting and it is often associated with laxative abuse. Community surveys have revealed that milder forms of both types of eating disorder are remarkably common in the general population (Fairburn and Hope, 1988).

Research evidence indicates that, although counselling can be effective for the underlying psychological problems in eating disorders, the abnormal eating behaviour itself tends to respond better to cognitive-behavioural interventions (Lacey, 1983). Family therapy (Will and Wrate, 1985) is often employed with some success in younger people who are still living in contact with their families. Alternatively, feminists have written widely about eating disorders (for example, Orbach, 1978) and a feminist perspective can be useful in understanding and helping within the counselling relationship. If progress is not being made, and the counsellor is not skilled in specific cognitive-behavioural interventions (challenging ideas about food and body image, keeping a diary of the behaviour, what appears to trigger it off and what its consequences are) the client should be encouraged to seek alternative help (usually referral to clinical psychology) via the GP. A history of anorexia nervosa, alcohol abuse or deliberate self-harm tends to indicate that treatment will be more complex.

Occasionally vomiting occurs without other symptoms of anorexia or bulimia. This so-called *psychogenic vomiting* can occur in severe anxiety. Rarely, this can lead to serious metabolic disturbances and requires involvement of the GP if not medical and/or psychiatric treatment.

## Sleep Problems

### Insomnia

Many things can cause difficulty in sleeping. Anxiety tends to cause difficulty in getting off to sleep. Depression is associated with waking through the night and being unable to get back to sleep and most markedly with waking early in the morning. In mania, the person hardly sleeps at all and so can gradually become quite exhausted. Drugs can interfere with sleep in a number of ways (see below) as can physical disorders.

### Sleeping Too Much

Some people complain of sleeping too much, feeling drowsy much of the time or suddenly falling asleep. This can occur in certain physical disorders, but common psychiatric causes can be sedatives or alcohol and depression. Drowsiness should not be confused with retardation (feeling slowed up but being perfectly awake) which has been discussed above.

## Sexual Problems

During counselling, sexual problems are often disclosed. The assessment and management of these problems are the subject of many excellent books, such as Kaplan (1987) or Hawton (1985). Here we simply discuss the presenting problems that may have serious medical or psychological relevance. Sexual deviations are often also included in a discussion of sexual disorders but these are rarely a presenting symptom of psychiatric illness.

### Loss of Desire

Although this may, rarely, have a physical cause it is most commonly associated with depression (when the onset might be quite sudden occurring in an otherwise satisfactory sexual relationship), other, more long-standing personality difficulties, or problems in a relationship.

### Loss of Arousal

In a male, this can have an underlying physical cause, especially certain kinds of medication. However, it also occurs in depression or anxiety and can be due to other underlying psychological factors which may or may not be connected to a particular relationship. Impotence caused by psychological factors can be situation-specific; that is, it only occurs with a particular partner, whereas early morning erections and masturbation are not affected. In women, failure of arousal is most likely to be psychological in cause, but lack of lubrication can have a physical basis – for example, during breastfeeding and after the menopause.

### Orgasm

In men, premature ejaculation is most likely to be psychological. Inability to ejaculate might be physical in origin and can be caused by drugs or neurological disturbance. Anorgasmia, or inability to experience an orgasm, is in women only rarely due to physical factors.

### Pain

Except in cases where there is a clear physical cause this is commonly psychological in origin in men. In women, spasm of the muscles preventing penetration (vaginismus) is almost always psychological in origin and related to anxiety about sex. Pain on intercourse or dyspareunia, is more often physical in cause.

### Pre-menstrual Syndrome (PMS)

The psychological symptoms of PMS include tension, irritability, depression, tiredness, sleep disturbance, mood swings and forgetfulness. Many women who complain of PMS actually are found, when they keep a diary of symptoms, to have symptoms throughout the month. Thus a complaint of PMS is often a more acceptable way of presenting with depression. Of particular relevance to the counselling setting is the observation that when women are depressed their mood is often markedly lower pre-menstrually. Many drug treatments have been tried but none has been demonstrated to be significantly effective for the majority of sufferers. More recently, cognitive-behavioural counselling approaches have been tried with some success (Blake et al., 1995). A small number of women (and their partners) complain of episodes of extreme irritability and violence in the pre-menstrual period. There has been a great deal of publicity relating this to low hormone levels and a suggestion (not backed by research) that this extreme state can be treated with drugs. In such a situation it would be important to check for other mental health problems (including personality problems) and relationship difficulties which could be exacerbating the condition before drawing the conclusion that this is 'pure' PMS. Physical and psychosocial aspects of PMS are also discussed in more detail on page 59 and psychological complications of the menopause on page 62.

### *Psychological Disturbances Associated with Pregnancy*

About 10 per cent of women develop post-natal depression in the first few weeks after the birth. These present with symptoms of depression (see page 61). A smaller number of women present with psychotic illnesses in the first two weeks after delivery. These may be depressive (about two-thirds) or schizophrenic in presentation. Health visitors play a key role in the detection of post-natal depression and in monitoring and support. Given the potential risk to the mother–child relationship if post-natal depression is not treated quickly, evidence of severity sufficient to meet the criteria for major depression requires the involvement of the GP to assess what form of treatment is appropriate.

Psychosocial aspects of pregnancy and childbirth are discussed in greater depth on page 60.

## Alcohol Problems

There are a number of factors that should raise suspicion of an alcohol problem (see the box on page 80). Alcohol problems require expert assessment when withdrawal or 'drying out' is being considered, and when the alcohol problem appears to be causing obvious mental or physical deterioration. This can be arranged via a GP or directly with a community alcohol team or local voluntary agency which deals with and assesses alcohol problems. These services can also provide simple advice and information on how to cut down consumption for clients who want this form of help. Clients with alcohol problems can benefit from counselling and some specific approaches which can help them successfully to change their behaviour, and prevent relapse, can be found in Davidson et al. (1991). Alcoholics Anonymous is the best-known community agency for alcohol problems. Members believe that alcoholism is a true medical disease which can only be treated by abstinence, and therefore people with lesser degrees of alcohol dependence who might benefit

**Features which Should Raise Suspicion of an Alcohol Problem**

*Physical*
Increasing consultation with GP about minor illnesses
Increasing absence rate from work due to sickness
High accident rate (including casualty attendances)
Recurrent minor gastrointestinal symptoms (e.g., gastritis, diarrhoea)
High blood pressure
Weight gain
Morning shakes
Alcohol on breath (especially in the mornings)

*Psychological*
Anxiety and depression
Increased aggression
Muddled thinking; forgetfulness
Jealousy: may be risk of violence to partner

*Social*
Deteriorating relationships
Deteriorating standards of dress and hygiene
Employment problems
Financial problems
Driving accidents/offences

from simply cutting down and learning how to control their drinking will not be accommodated. Nevertheless, many people get a great deal of support from AA and its sister organisations Al-Anon (for spouses of drinkers) and Al-Ateen (for teenage children of drinkers) and all can be contacted via the telephone directory.

## Drug Problems

Factors that should raise suspicion of a drug problem are shown in the box on page 81.

Drugs have two types of effects: those that are associated with intoxication and those associated with withdrawal (see Table 4.1).

There is insufficient space to do this topic full justice here. *Drug Scenes* (Royal College of Psychiatrists, 1987) provides an excellent introduction. Almost all areas now have specialist counselling

---

**Features which Should Raise Suspicion of a Drug Problem**

*Physical*
Listlessness
Rashes
Drowsiness
Change in pupil size
Needle marks
Smell (solvents)

*Psychological*
Odd behaviour
Increased aggression
Muddled thinking, forgetfulness, confusion

*Social*
Deteriorating relationships
Deteriorating standards of dress and hygiene
Employment problems
Financial problems

---

agencies, both statutory (Community Drugs Teams) and voluntary (such as Drugline) which can provide invaluable support and guidance. Drug agencies can also provide information about HIV prevention and needle exchange services. Possession of most of the drugs below is illegal, apart from some of the opiates which are used for analgesia and solvents which can be bought over the counter. In general, counsellors should be cautious when managing people with drug problems and employ clear contracts, setting limits on what will or will not be acceptable if counselling is to continue. Specific approaches to counselling people with drug problems are discussed in Bennett (1990). It would generally be wise to avoid taking on such clients if the counsellor is working entirely in independent private practice.

### Violent Behaviour

Violent behaviour is not uncommonly associated with personality disorder, where there is likely to be a long history of similar events. Violent incidents sometimes occur when people are under the influence of alcohol and drugs and this may also be associated

**Table 4.1** *Effects of commonly used drugs*

| Drug | Intoxication | Withdrawal |
|---|---|---|
| **Opiates** (sedative analgesic) e.g. Heroin (smoked, inhaled, injected) Methadone (used in treatment) morphine, codeine tablets, *DF118* tablets, pethidine, *Diconal* | Drowsiness, relaxation, small pupils, constipation | Agitation, sweats, diarrhoea, big pupils, yawning, goose flesh, stomach cramps |
| **Cocaine** (stimulant) Sniffed or injected 'Crack' cocaine especially potent | Euphoria, excitement Can cause paranoid psychosis | Mild, but profound psychological dependence develops* |
| **Amphetamine** (stimulant) Tablets or injection | Excitement, loss of appetite, increased energy Can cause psychosis | Depression, fatigue, headache |
| **LSD** (hallucinogenic) Oral | Change in perception 'Bad trips' Can cause psychosis | None, but flashbacks occur |
| **Cannabis** (milder hallucinogenic, used widely) Marijuana, hash, dope. Smoked or in food or drink | Euphoria, relaxation, perceptual changes Can precipitate psychosis in those susceptible | None, but psychological dependence* develops |
| **Sedatives** e.g. barbiturates (oral, injected), benzodiazepines (temazepam widely injected) *Heminevrin* (used in alcohol withdrawal but also abused) | Relaxation, slurred speech, drowsiness. Barbiturates and *Heminevrin* cause death in overdose. | Anxiety, tremor, delirium, fits. |
| **Solvents** (not only abused by young people) e.g. paint, lighter fuel, glue | Euphoria, drowsiness, confusion Brain, liver and kidney damage. Death by toxic effects or suffocation (plastic bags) | None, but psychological dependence* develops |
| **Ecstasy** 'Designer drug' widely used by young people in association with 'raves' | Feelings of euphoria and well-being. Can cause depression, panic disorder, psychosis | None, but flashbacks can occur |

* constant desire to use.
Proprietary (Brand) names in italics.

with personality disorder. Where violence is threatened towards partners or spouses there is often evidence of morbid jealousy. This can be identified when jealousy dominates a spouse's every thought and action. Morbidly jealous husbands follow their wives around and cannot be re-assured. They may check their underwear for stains, misinterpret events as indicators of unfaithfulness and put unreasonable constraints on their partners which cause great distress. It is often associated with alcoholism but can also occur in other forms of psychiatric illness. If violent behaviour is identified, the safety of the spouse is paramount as it can be a cause of serious and often homicidal domestic violence.

Depression can be associated with violence, not only suicide but also homicidal acts, often against the person's family followed by suicide. ***Threats must be taken seriously.*** If a client makes such a threat it must not be assumed that this will not be carried out. Other professionals may need to be involved to assess fully the situation. This is a situation where absolute confidentiality should be questioned.

In mania, violence may erupt when an irritable manic person is thwarted. Finally, violent episodes do occur in people with schizophrenia but are uncommon. They are often unprovoked and may seem senseless to someone with no knowledge of the person's inner world. In the context of counselling, if a relative who is being counselled reports episodes of hostility and irritability and feels afraid, their fears should be taken seriously. There is insufficient space here to discuss all the ways in which transgressions against the law (common examples which a counsellor might come into contact with are shoplifting and criminal damage) can indicate the presence of psychiatric illness. ***Where there is any threat of violence the assessment of the mental health service must be sought unless the counsellor is absolutely clear there is no evidence of mental illness.***

## Odd Speech

*Slowing Down or Speeding Up*
In severe depression, due to psychomotor retardation, speech can be very markedly slowed down. The opposite to this is so-called 'pressure of speech' which may occur to some degree in people who are excited or anxious but becomes very marked in

psychotic illness, particularly *hypomania*. As speech becomes faster (reflecting faster and faster thoughts), the ideas seem to become disconnected although in fact there are still associations between them. This occurs in *mania* and is called 'flight of ideas'. (The features of mania and hypomania are discussed further below.) It must be distinguished from over-inclusiveness, which occurs when someone talks a great deal, keeps straying from the point to tell some related story but does eventually return to the original thread. This is usually a feature of abnormal personality (particularly obsessive-compulsive; see Appendix 8, page 134).

### Speech which is Difficult to Make Sense of
In *flight of ideas*, speech appears to jump rapidly from topic to topic, but if you write down an example of such speech you can usually find that there are connections. It occurs in mania, usually in association with pressure of speech. If speech is very difficult to follow indeed and seems to make no sense, this might possibly be *schizophrenic thought disorder*, in which the person jumps from topic to topic and there are no connections and no associated pressure of speech. The first time you experience this you think that you aren't somehow trying hard enough to ask the right questions and it can take a moment or two to realise that you simply haven't got a clue what the person is talking about!

### Saying Very Little or Having Too Much to Say
In both depression and schizophrenia there may be so-called *poverty of speech*. In depression this is again related to psycho-motor retardation. In schizophrenia it can be a result of preoccupation with strange experiences. Having too much to say is not in itself a symptom of mental illness, but in schizophrenic thought disorder the person sometimes becomes *over-inclusive*. This is not a simple matter of digressing from the topic at hand which often occurs normally, but is much more pervasive, as the person does not see that they have strayed from the point and that what they are saying is in fact irrelevant to it.

## Strange Ideas

### Not Feeling in Control of your own Thoughts
People suffering from schizophrenia can experience the frightening feeling that they are no longer in full control of their thoughts.

**Table 4.2**   *Symptoms of schizophrenia*

**'Schneider's first rank symptoms' occur in acute illness**
Hearing one's thoughts spoken aloud within one's head
Hearing voices commenting on one's actions
Experiences that someone or something is influencing one's body
Thought broadcasting/insertion/withdrawal
Delusional perception
Any feeling or action which is experienced as influenced by others

In **chronic** illnesses a number of other symptoms/signs may also be present:
   social isolation or withdrawal
   impairment in occupational or social functioning
   poor self-care
   limited range of emotional expression
   muddled thinking (thought disorder)

They may feel that their own thoughts can be experienced by other people at the same time ('I don't need to tell you what I'm thinking because you know already'). This is known as *thought broadcasting*. A related experience is *thought insertion*, which is the experience that other people's thoughts are being placed in your mind or that thoughts are being removed from your mind, which is called *thought withdrawal.* There is no simple checklist by which to diagnose schizophrenia. If there is any evidence of delusions, hallucinations, incoherence or grossly disorganised behaviour, ***referral to the mental health services is essential.*** A number of symptoms are, however, characteristically associated with an *acute onset* of a schizophrenic illness and are known as *Schneider's First Rank Symptoms* after the doctor who first described them.

*Delusions*
Psychiatrists have spent many years finding new ways of classifying delusions. Basically a delusion is a false belief, not shared by others of the same cultural group, which is firmly held and cannot be dispelled by argument or proof to the contrary. A delusion might coincidentally be true, but the logical basis from which the belief is derived is at fault. For example, a woman believes that her husband is having an affair and this may indeed be true, but when asked, she explains that her belief is based on his preference for a particular type of breakfast cereal!

It is worth differentiating delusions from *over-valued ideas*, which are deeply held personal convictions held with less conviction than delusions, sometimes understandable in terms of mood or life experiences, and *ideas of reference*, which occur in sensitive people who are prone to feel that people take undue notice of them or that events have a special significance for them.

Sometimes delusions arrive fully formed 'out of the blue' (*sudden delusional ideas*) or they sometimes occur after a period of apparent perplexity when the person feels that something strange is going on but can't quite work out what it is (*delusional mood*). A *delusional perception* occurs when the person attaches a delusional meaning to a normal observation and this meaning cannot be understood in terms of the person's mood. For example, a person who has felt uneasy for some days and is in no way elated in mood sees a crack in a window pane and suddenly realises that he is Jesus Christ. All these delusional experiences which do not seem to be understandable in terms of the person's underlying mood are characteristic of schizophrenia. However, other types of delusions, which are understandable, occur in both depression and mania (for example, a depressed person experiencing pain and believing that he is dying of cancer).

Delusions can be about all sorts of things. Most people are familiar with the idea of paranoid or persecutory delusions, but delusions can also be concerned with feeling controlled by someone else or believing that things going on around you in people's conversations or on TV refer to you (delusions of reference). Delusions may also have a religious content, or be concerned with infidelity or love (believing that someone is in love with you). They can also be grandiose (believing you are special in some way), depressive (concerned with feelings of guilt, worthlessness or hopelessness), hypochondriacal (concerned with belief in bodily illness) or nihilistic (believing that parts of one's body do not exist).

*Kathy visits Henry, a counsellor in private practice, and complains of depression. They work on this for a while, then Kathy stops coming, telling Henry that she can't leave her home. Henry agrees to visit Kathy at home. There she tells Henry that she is being watched, there is a campaign of psychological terror against her and she asks Henry to continue to visit her at home. Henry learns that Kathy has seen a psychiatrist and a social worker, has tried medication that appears to have no effect, and is regarded as a long-term 'case' to be managed in the community. Kathy and Henry get on well and Henry is reluctant to stop seeing Kathy in a supportive capacity. Is this a good idea?*

Comment: *Yes, as long as Henry is clear and honest in his contract with Kathy about what he can and cannot do to help her. His supportive relationship is clearly valued. He should encourage Kathy to tell those who are involved in her care that she is seeing Henry and if there is any clear deterioration in Kathy's mental state this will be particularly essential. He will not be able, within the bounds of the confidential relationship, to inform Kathy's other professional carers without Kathy's permission. If, however, he becomes concerned for Kathy's safety he may have to reconsider his responsibilities in discussion with his own supervisor. He must ensure that he keeps full and accurate records of his contacts with Kathy.*

Delusions occur in all types of major psychiatric illness; that is, in schizophrenia, mania, depression and organic brain disease. Clear evidence of delusional ideas requires referral to the mental health services for assessment and it is unnecessary to go into the details of differential diagnosis here. There are, however, one or two simple rules to bear in mind if needed. In the major mood disorders (depression and mania) the delusions are usually understandable from the underlying mood (for example, believing that you are dying if you are depressed, grandiose delusions in mania), and other features of mood disorder will be present. In schizophrenia the beliefs are not understandable in terms of the underlying mood, and other symptoms such as those described earlier may be present. In organic brain disease other features such as confusion or memory problems will be found.

### Obsessions and Compulsions

Obsessions can take the form of a thought, feeling or impulse which the person tries to resist, and realises is clearly out of keeping with his or her own personality. These are sometimes associated with compulsions, which are acts (sometimes called 'rituals') which the person feels compelled to carry out. Obsessional thoughts can take the form of a persistent rumination which is perceived to be senseless, for example, a mother thinking 'my child will get sick and die because I've fed her the wrong sort of babyfood' even though she logically knows that this is not the case. Common compulsive acts include cleaning and handwashing because of a fear of contamination, and checking by counting things over and over again or checking door locks several times. Some people have obsessional personalities and their problems are lifelong, but obsessional symptoms can become worse particularly in association with depression. Obsessional thoughts are difficult to treat, but, if associated with depression, they often disappear as this is treated or respond to anti-depressant medication. Compulsions also may respond to behavioural treatment. Obsessional symptoms can benefit from referral to a psychiatrist or clinical psychologist, so assessment should be discussed with the client but is only essential when the condition is very disabling or clearly associated with major depression. Generally, there is no evidence that talking therapies help people with pure obsessional illnesses but they can help the associated depression.

*Gail sees a client, Bridget, in an agency where time limits are imposed on all clients. Bridget reveals in the third session that she has some seriously compulsive behaviour – checking locks and electrical appliances in particular, but wants Gail's help. Gail believes that Bridget needs an experienced behaviour therapist but has difficulty finding one, and Bridget anyway says she wants to continue with Gail. What can or should Gail do?*

Comment: *This depends on a number of things. How long has the compulsive behaviour been going on for? What was the problem with which Bridget originally presented for counselling? Is there any evidence that Bridget is depressed? If the behaviour is long-standing, it would be entirely appropriate to spend some time clarifying with Bridget exactly what her difficulties are and organising a referral through her GP to the clinical psychology services even if this takes some time. If there is any evidence of depression, particularly if the compulsive behaviour has arisen or become worse since the onset, it would be worthwhile trying to persuade Bridget to see her GP for treatment. In the meantime, Gail can work with Bridget on her other presenting problems, which may be exacerbating her compulsive problem by leading to increased tension and anxiety, and provide appropriate support.*

## Strange Experiences

*Hallucinations* must be distinguished from *illusions*. Illusions occur when actual stimuli are falsely perceived; for example, in a dark room misidentifying a hat stand for a man waiting to jump. Illusions commonly occur when people are anxious or fearful. Hallucinations are perceived as being real but occur in the absence of any real external stimulus, so truly 'hearing voices which are not there'. Hallucinations can occur in any of the sensory modalities – hearing, sight, smell, taste or touch. Hallucinations occur in schizophrenia, depression, mania, organic brain diseases and drug-induced states.

It can be difficult to distinguish true hallucinations from other experiences such as 'out of the body' states and religious experiences (James, 1960). A general rule is that many such 'transpersonal' experiences are welcome and not perceived as frightening or alien in any way, which is not the case in most mental illnesses. An exception would be, for example, hallucinations occurring in someone in a state of mania who experiences 'hearing the voice of God' in a state of intense, elated mood. Therefore it is important not just to look at these experiences but other aspects of the person's state and functioning.

Transient hallucinations can, however, occur in normal people, often when falling asleep or just in the state of waking up. These are not necessarily of any significance but any persistent hallucinations indicate need for assessment by the mental health services.

## Changes in Mood

Mood problems will be a common presenting complaint in counselling clients. Occasionally mood abnormalities can be an indicator of more serious psychiatric illness or indeed physical illness.

### Anxiety

Anxiety can be caused by an overactive thyroid gland, certain types of hormonal tumours and epilepsy. Anxiety is a very common symptom, which can be present to a degree in many types of problem (as well as in almost everyone). However, when severe, it is often associated with alcohol problems or tranquilliser

**Table 4.3**   *Symptoms of anxiety*

| Physical symptoms of anxiety | Psychological symptoms of anxiety |
| --- | --- |
| Palpitations | Sense of anxiety or fear |
| Breathlessness | Difficulty sleeping |
| Chest pain | Difficulty concentrating |
| Headache | Irritability |
| Tingling sensations | Fear of impending doom |
| Trembling | Feelings of unreality |
| Tiredness and fatigue | |
| Sweating | |
| Hot flushes | |
| Dry mouth | |
| Frequency (constantly wanting to pass urine) | |

dependence when these substances have been used in an attempt to combat the symptoms. Anxiety is commonly associated with depression, and worry about the physical symptoms of anxiety (see Table 4.3) can lead to concern about possible physical illness (*hypochondriasis*) and subsequent unnecessary negative investigations which only lead to further preoccupation about its presence.

Psychiatrists recognise different types of anxiety. The only relevance to the counsellor is to know that particular types of anxiety have been demonstrated to respond well to behavioural treatments. This is true for specific phobias (such as snake phobia, fear of spiders) and agoraphobia. Also there is evidence that panic disorder, which is episodes of panic often associated with agoraphobia and/or depression, responds to anti-depressant treatment. Episodes of panic can often be helped by simple breathing exercises and distraction techniques. Generalised anxiety, which means feeling anxious most of the time, can be helped by relaxation exercises and problem solving, and here alternative therapies such as hypnotherapy and yoga techniques may help in addition to more traditional, progressive muscular relaxation training which is commonly available in the form of audiotape instruction. However, just because a person is undergoing a desensitisation programme with the community psychiatric nurse for her agoraphobia, it does not mean that she would also not benefit from a counselling intervention to help her explore the underlying problems that have led to the onset of the symptoms.

Post-Traumatic Stress Disorder (PTSD; see box on page 92) is a recently described syndrome which occurs after people have been exposed to major stressful events outside the range of normal human experience. Recent evidence suggests that it can be effectively treated but that it may be a somewhat more complex syndrome than originally thought and there is often considerable overlap with personality disorder, unresolved grief, depression, phobic anxiety, drug or alcohol abuse. Simple 'debriefing' involves asking exactly what happened, allowing the client to describe and re-live the experience and associated emotions. It is also important to help the client to explore the meaning and significance of the event to them. If this is not successful it may be necessary to refer on to someone with particular experience and expertise. Specialist cognitive-behavioural approaches to counselling in this disorder are described in Scott and Stradling (1992).

*A counsellor, Tom, has referred to him a client, George, who has witnessed a death at work. The brief training that Tom had in PTSD stressed the need for early intervention and active encouragement of George to re-experience the event. When he follows this path George begins to experience panic attacks. What should Tom do?*

Comment: *Tom should reassess the problem fully and clarify in much more depth what the meaning of the event for George might be. There may be painful associations with past personal events or other concomitant stresses and difficulties in George's life which George may not be ready or able to address at this point and may require more in-depth psychotherapeutic help. What support exists for George? Is there any evidence of depression, risk of suicide or substance misuse? How much of an impact is the problem having on normal life? Is the panic linked to avoidance of places or people with painful associations?*

Clinical psychologists are particularly skilled in the detailed assessment and non-drug treatment of severe anxiety disorders. If anxiety is very severe, the client should be encouraged to seek the GP's opinion to ensure that physical causes are ruled out. Specific forms of anxiety such as panic disorder and phobias benefit from assessment and possibly treatment by a clinical

---

**Post-Traumatic Stress Disorder**

Experienced event outside the range of usual human experience that would be markedly distressing to almost anyone, e.g., serious threat to life, seeing another person killed.

Event is persistently re-experienced, e.g., by flashbacks, dreams. Distress when reminded of the event.

Persistent avoidance of stimuli associated with the trauma or numbing of general responsiveness.

Persistent symptoms of arousal, e.g., sleep problems, irritability, anger, poor concentration, physical symptoms of anxiety when exposed to stimulus that reminds of the event.

Onset may be delayed.

Duration of symptoms for at least one month.

---

psychologist, behavioural nurse or a suitably trained CPN. Depression and anxiety commonly occur together and treatment of the underlying depression is often effective in dealing with the symptoms of anxiety. Consider whether major depression is present and, if so, consider asking the client to see the GP.

*Depression*
Depression can be caused by drugs or physical illness. This form of *secondary depression* can be difficult to distinguish from a psychological illness. Important early clues could be signs of organic mental illness such as disorientation or forgetfulness, particularly if these fluctuate. Some drugs and physical illnesses that can cause depression are listed below (Table 4.4). This is not an exhaustive list and, if you have a suspicion that these may be a factor, follow it up by asking about drugs and illness and if you are in any doubt at all suggest a consultation with the GP.

However, depressive symptoms will be amongst those most commonly encountered by the counsellor. From a psychiatric viewpoint, it is important to recognise depression of a severity to be called *Major Depression*, which roughly translates as 'clinical depression' (see the box on page 94).

**Table 4.4**   *Pharmacological and physical causes of depression*

| Some drugs which can cause depression |
| --- |
| Reserpine |
| Beta blockers |
| Barbiturates |
| Indomethacin |
| Steroids and the contraceptive pill |
| Withdrawal from amphetamines and appetite suppressants |
| Ecstasy |
| L-Dopa |
| Phenytoin |
| Certain drugs used in chemotherapy for cancer. |

| Some physical illnesses which can cause depression |
| --- |
| Dementia |
| Brain tumour |
| Parkinson's disease |
| Multiple sclerosis |
| Influenza |
| Glandular fever |
| Vitamin deficiencies |
| Thyroid disease |
| Various forms of cancer. |

Depression may be indistinguishable from abnormal grief, which occurs when the normal grieving process which occurs after bereavement becomes blocked. Counselling strategies applicable in dealing with grief are described by Worden (1991). If there are also clear symptoms of major depression, a consultation with the GP should be advised.

There is evidence that major depression responds quickly to anti-depressant medication in 70–80 per cent of cases. This will be irrelevant if the person has a strong preference for treatment by counselling, but if there is clear evidence of deterioration or a failure to respond to therapy discuss referral to the GP and/or the mental health service. Some people who are depressed cannot make the best use of counselling interventions until they have received anti-depressant medication because of their slowed and muddled thinking brought about by psychomotor retardation. *Treatment with anti-depressants therefore does not in any way preclude counselling, and a combination of the two can be highly*

---

**Major Depression**

*Presence of*
Depressed mood and/or loss of interest or pleasure
plus at least four of:

Agitation or retardation (slowing up)
Loss of energy or fatigue
Loss of interest or pleasure or loss of libido
Feeling of worthlessness or guilt
Thoughts of death/suicidal thoughts
Change in appetite or weight (increased or decreased)
Sleep difficulties (too little or too much).

Present for at least two weeks

---

*effective*. There is as yet no clear research evidence that person-centred counselling or psychodynamic psychotherapy can be effective specifically in major depression, but there is evidence for the effectiveness of Cognitive-Behavioural Therapy (CBT) and InterPersonal Therapy (IPT). IPT is hardly known in the United Kingdom yet but is more common in the United States and focuses on social functioning and relationships. Psychological treatments are reviewed in Paykel and Priest (1992), and Problem-Solving therapy has also recently been demonstrated to be as effective as anti-depressant treatment (Mynors-Wallis, 1995). The severity of depression can be monitored with simple rating scales filled in by the client. The best-known of these is the Beck Depression Inventory – see France and Robson (1986) – which is very acceptable to clients and sensitive to change over time. In very severe depression the ideas of worthlessness become delusional ideas and there may also be other depressive delusions and even auditory or visual hallucinations. *In the presence of such symptoms* **referral to the mental health services is essential.**

There are two major groups of anti-depressants now in use, of which the *tricyclic* anti-depressants have been in use for nearly 40 years and are still used by many GPs and psychiatrists, and the *Serotonin Re-uptake Inhibitors (SSRIs)* (which include Prozac) which are much newer. The two groups have very different side effects. There are also the *MAOIs (MonoAmine Oxidase Inhibitors)*, which were unfashionable for many years because of dietary restrictions necessary when taking them. A new MAOI called moclobemide is, however, available now, which does not require all of these restrictions. Some people may also be taking lithium, which is used either in combination with anti-depressants to make them work more effectively or to prevent further episodes of depression. All anti-depressants take at least two to three weeks to work before they start to have an effect on mood and it is during this period that the side effects are most apparent. During this time, however, people taking tricyclic drugs will usually begin to sleep better and feel calmer. This is not the case with the SSRIs, which do not promote sleep. Prozac has received more publicity than the other new drugs and has been variously claimed as a wonder drug (Kramer, 1994), and to cause suicide amongst people taking it. There is no evidence for either claim, but it can cause people to feel more agitated, and if this is clearly a problem the person should be encouraged to see their GP. If a client is clearly severely depressed but hostile to any idea of medication it is important to negotiate clearly what one is prepared and able to offer, to inform about what can be helpful in such circumstances and to try and negotiate a compromise – for example, to try counselling first – but if there is any further marked deterioration the client will consider medication. At the very least in such circumstances the client should be asked to consult the GP, and the counsellor should attempt to negotiate that he or she is kept closely informed of progress.

ECT (Electro-convulsive therapy) tends now only to be used in very severe depression when the person becomes stuporose, which means completely mute, immobile and not eating or drinking, or when there is a very severe suicidal risk and it is dangerous to wait for anti-depressants to begin to work. Before the electric current is applied the person is anaesthetised and completely relaxed. They wake within a few minutes and have a brief period of memory loss and a headache. Some people, however, do complain of longer-term memory difficulties after ECT.

Suicide is a major risk in the treatment of depression and the management of this risk by the counsellor will be dealt with below.

### Excitement

Overexcitement can occur in mania. It can also be caused by organic brain disease. *Mania* (see the box on page 96) often goes

---

**Mania**

*Presence of*
Elated or irritable mood
plus at least three of:

Overactivity
Increased talkativeness or pressure of speech
Flight of ideas or racing thoughts
Distractibility
Grandiosity (including grandiose delusions)
Indiscreet behaviour with poor judgement
Decreased sleep

Present for at least one week (or any duration if hospitalised)

---

unrecognised, and in its milder form (hypomania) can be simply mistaken for 'bad' behaviour or an irritable personality.

In mania, mood becomes elevated. When this occurs in someone who also has a history of depression it is called manic-depressive illness. The manic person often describes their mood as 'on top of the world' and 'marvellous'. At first the humour they display may have an infectious quality and it is easy to find oneself laughing along. Later, frustration of grandiose plans to change the world can lead to irritability and aggression and the manic person sometimes gets into trouble with the law. Occasionally, a mixture of depressive and manic symptoms are found together. This is known as a *mixed affective state*. As in depression, mania can also be caused by a variety of drugs and physical illnesses. These will not be dealt with here as it should be clear that mania of any cause does require medical investigation and treatment and any form of counselling intervention on its own will not be effective. ***Referral to the mental health services for assessment is indicated, and this should be arranged as urgently as possible before the situation deteriorates further.***

In the acute phase, mania is treated with major tranquillisers; for example, chlorpromazine (*Largactil*), haloperidol (*Haldol*). In the longer term, manic-depressive episodes can be prevented with lithium (*Priadel, Camcolit*) or carbamezepine (*Tegretol*). Mania and schizophrenia are often confused with each other and the differentiation is often not very clear cut. Illnesses which have features of both manic-depressive illness and schizophrenia are sometimes given the name *schizoaffective* and a combination of treatment is used.

Excitement also occurs in other forms of psychiatric disorder, including dementia, epilepsy, schizophrenia, organic confusional states and other types of organic brain disease. Significant excitement of any form which has any features suggestive of mental illness **requires urgent assessment,** in the first instance by the GP if there are features suggestive of a physical cause.

## Confusion and Forgetfulness

### Confusion

Confusion can mean all sorts of things. When psychiatrists use the word it usually means *disorientation*. This means having difficulty with remembering who you are, the name of the person you are with, what time it is (time, day, date, month or year). In acute brain disease (also known as *delirium*), the person is disorientated and also has a fluctuating conscious level, drifting in and out of full awareness. This sort of 'confusion' should be distinguished from that of someone who is depressed who has difficulty thinking clearly, the more insidious difficulties related to forgetfulness seen in chronic brain diseases, and from *thought disorder* and *perplexity* seen in schizophrenia and mania. The presence of 'confusion' indicates that **medical investigation is required urgently,** as many disorders which present with a picture of acute organic brain disease can be reversible if treated quickly and may also be life threatening (for example, drug intoxications, alcohol withdrawal, infections such as encephalitis or meningitis, cardiovascular disease).

### Forgetfulness

Many people complain of forgetfulness. When people are very anxious they sometimes seem forgetful, but on testing it is clear that their concentration is so impaired that they have difficulty attending to and registering new memories. In depression, memory sometimes seems impaired for a similar reason and also because of slowed-up thinking. More severe memory impairment is seen in chronic organic brain diseases such as *dementia* (where the forgetfulness is usually associated with other features such as impaired intellectual performance and disorientation). People who have experienced head injuries may have long-lasting memory problems. Alcohol abuse is another common cause of this problem. The dementia associated with AIDS is discussed in Chapter 3.

## Physical Symptoms

It is not unusual for psychiatric illness to present with physical symptoms. Clearly, if a client is presenting new and worrying physical symptoms to you it will be necessary to encourage them to seek medical advice. However, it is important to mention here the situations in which physical symptoms do not denote an underlying physical disorder as the counsellor may become involved in the care of a person in which physical symptoms are a presenting feature of underlying psychological distress. This phenomenon is known as *somatisation*. This is very commonly seen by GPs (Gask, 1995). Many people are unhappy about talking about emotional problems to doctors for a number of reasons, one of the most important of which is the stigma of mental illness. Sometimes people go to the doctor to complain about the physical symptoms that accompany emotional illness, such as palpitations caused by anxiety or weight loss caused by depression. Sometimes people become preoccupied with the worry or fear that they have a serious physical illness (known as *hypochondriasis*). If the depression or anxiety is missed, and the symptoms are investigated, this can further convince the person that they do have an underlying physical disorder. When the GP tries to help the patient to accept a psychological view of their problems, it may then be more difficult than it might have been earlier. A useful practical model for managing somatisation in primary care which is of help to both GPs and counsellors is described in Goldberg et al. (1989), and deals with engaging people in talking about emotional as well as physical symptoms and helping them to make links between the two.

The counsellor could become involved in this problem, particularly when working in a medical setting when the GP refers the patient. It may take some time to engage such a client in talking about emotions. It is important to liaise closely with the GP to discuss how to respond to physical complaints and clarify the GP's continuous role in the client's physical care and investigations. It is important to try and avoid adopting a stance whereby, for example, a counsellor working in a medical setting might get into conflict with the GP about whether further investigations or treatment are necessary. Such a scenario would possibly suggest issues relating to overidentification which should be explored in supervision. The most difficult area will lie around illnesses such as ME, about which doctors themselves disagree. However, even if the counsellor believes that the client is not getting the right treatment, he or she should try to avoid stepping into the role of advising further interventions and especially acting as the client's advocate with their GP. A problem occurs if the counsellor is employed in an agency where he or she is also expected to act in an advocacy role. The problems inherent in combining these roles are discussed on page 107.

## Some Special Topics

### *Which Psychiatric Conditions Might be Exacerbated by Counselling?*

There has been considerable research in psychotherapy into factors associated with a poor outcome (Lambert et al., 1986). There are strong indications that more severely disturbed people (particularly those who are 'psychotic' and those who could be described as 'borderline') do less well in psychotherapy. 'Borderline' is a term commonly used by psychotherapists (but less by psychiatrists) to describe a condition characterised by unstable relationships with others, often of an intense, short-term nature, impulsive behaviour, and brief periods of depression associated with suicidal behaviour. Many of these people also abuse alcohol and drugs and some also experience brief episodes in which they do lose touch with reality and experience psychotic symptoms. These people cause a great deal of anxiety in both general practice and psychiatric settings but are often deemed unsuitable for formal, insight-orientated psychotherapy or counselling. They seem to respond better to a more limited supportive commitment over a long period of time, although recent work has suggested that cognitive analytic therapy (CAT) may be helpful (Ryle and Beard, 1993).

Some particularly aggressive styles or models of therapy which are confrontational may also break down necessary defences in someone who otherwise appears to be coping with everyday life, at least superficially.

*Susan is a counsellor in training who chooses for her personal therapist a Gestalt counsellor. All goes well until Susan is encouraged to voice very distressed feelings, following which she seems to plunge into very confused states of mind. The counsellor says this must be worked through but Susan is afraid – she seems to feel worse and at times cannot cope with everyday routines.*

Comment: *If Susan feels afraid – confused, and is having difficulty maintaining a sense of the integrity of her everyday life, this is an important warning sign that she is not coping with the therapy. The therapist should heed these warning signs and discuss the problem with her own supervisor. Perhaps the exploratory process needs to be taken at a gentler pace, or possibly the Gestalt approach is too confrontational for Susan to cope with at this point. Susan should discuss her worries both with her counsellor and her own trainer. The possibility exists that Susan should not proceed with her own counselling training if the counselling process is threatening her own sense of integrity of 'self' in this way. She may benefit from assessment from a suitably well-experienced and qualified psychodynamic psychotherapist.*

If a counsellor becomes involved in the care of someone with severe or 'borderline' personality difficulties it is crucially important that he or she is absolutely clear what the purpose, boundaries and limitations of the proposed sessions actually are. It is extremely easy to get unwittingly into a regressive relationship with such a client. Some therapists controversially encourage regression as part of the treatment they offer (Berke, 1979). In supervised insight-orientated therapy this may be entirely appropriate, but for a counsellor aiming to offer a brief intervention to enable the client to deal more effectively with current life problems this will be counter-productive. In some people who have a tenuous grip on reality, such as in 'borderline' personality disorder, the regression can become pathological and perhaps result in further disintegration or acting out of destructive feelings both inside and outside the counselling sessions. Clearly, these issues must be addressed in assessment and supervision. Although many such clients are assessed as unsuitable for psychotherapy by mental health services, a counsellor can have a role to play in management as long as sessions are suitably tailored to the client's needs.

One would not deny the importance of support and understanding for the person who is presenting with symptoms of schizophrenia, nor deny that the presenting delusions and hallucinatory voices may be, like dreams, a reflection of thoughts and fears. However, the arousal caused by potentially uncovering material with which the disturbed person may not be able to work and use has led to a generally accepted belief that counselling is contra-indicated other than at a supportive level. Specific *cognitive-behavioural* methods for helping people who hear voices or experience delusional ideas are now coming into wider psychological practice but require considerable skilled training and supervision and are beyond the scope of this book.

If a client is particularly keen to try these psychological methods, it would be appropriate to try and ***arrange referral to a suitably trained clinical psychologist*** but this would be best carried out in conjunction with the client's GP if this is possible.

Counsellors sometimes find that, rather than working with the person suffering from schizophrenia they are helping a parent or spouse to come to terms with what can be a devastating family problem, and in doing so, it is hoped, helping to dispel the myth that the illness is in some way the 'fault' of the family. Although there is certainly no doubt that tension within the family can increase the likelihood of an acute relapse (by mechanisms not dissimilar to that by which therapy may cause this), the concept of a 'schizophrenogenic family' described by Laing and others in the 1960s (Laing and Esterson, 1970) has no basis in fact.

The other group of people who could be described as severely disturbed are those with severe depression and manic-depressive illness. In both of these states it is important to recognise the early signs of deterioration. People with depression commonly seek, and benefit from, counselling, but there is no evidence for the efficacy of any form of psychological treatment in very severe depression. In both severe depression and mania the impact on thinking processes of the condition (in depression thinking is slowed down, and in mania it is speeded up, the effect of both is to reduce concentration) make it increasingly difficult to work through processes coherently in the way that is required in counselling. There is actually the risk that the severely depressed person will be disheartened by his or her failure to make progress and view this as more evidence of his or her deteriorating mental ability, which might be wrongly ascribed to dementia, or feel guilty for taking up the counsellor's time. In any event, counselling might, unless these signs are detected and the style altered to a more supportive one, be at the least perceived as a negative experience and at worst be potentially harmful – personal accounts are fascinating; see Styron (1992) and Sutherland (1987).

Those with manic-depressive illness can benefit from counselling but there is no evidence that this will decrease the likelihood of a relapse in their illness, whereas drug treatments have been demonstrated by research to prevent relapse. In both cases it is important to discuss with the client what he or she may be expected to gain from counselling and the need to talk over as a separate issue, with the GP or psychiatrist as appropriate, the need to stay on medication. Counselling may potentially cause deterioration in both these conditions by delaying reassessment by the GP during the completion of the agreed number of sessions. The counsellor can be alert to and aware of potential signs of deterioration and in particular, with worsening depression, must be conscious of and ask about suicidal risk.

### Helping a Client to Withdraw from Tranquillisers

Many people in the community are dependent on minor tranquillisers. Counselling interventions have been demonstrated to decrease prescriptions for these drugs and play an important part in the management of anxiety in primary care. The counsellor might be involved in helping the person who is dependent arrive at an informed decision about whether or not to attempt withdrawal and then supporting them through that process while they learn to face up to anxiety again, and learn to deal with it in other, healthier ways. Withdrawal means facing up to oneself again and learning how to cope with life difficulties. Withdrawal regimes should be drawn up in conjunction with a GP or CPN. The person may decide initially to switch from a short-acting drug to a longer acting one such as Valium, before withdrawing, which is often easier for some than for others. See guidelines produced by the Mental Health Foundation (1992) for a medical viewpoint and Hammersley (1995) for an excellent introduction to counselling aspects.

### Responding to Suicidal Ideas

The ethical and legal issues involved in dealing with a client's suicidal ideas have been addressed elsewhere in this book (see

Chapter 5). From a psychiatric point of view, suicide is seen as essentially preventable if the person is suffering from a treatable mental illness such that the suicidal ideation would no longer be expressed if the person received and responded to treatment adequately. The majority of people who successfully complete suicide are suffering from depression (around 70–80 per cent), a smaller proportion (about 15 per cent) from alcohol dependence and the remainder is made up by those with schizophrenic illnesses, personality disorders, drug misuse and finally no psychiatric disorder. In the past the majority of people who committed suicide had contact with their GP in the month before the suicide but this is no longer the case, and the largest 'growth area' is now in young men who have much less contact with statutory agencies and tend to be less likely to be 'clinically' depressed. It is for the individual practitioner to decide, in consultation with his supervisor, when to respect the wishes of a client who does not want any (usually further) psychiatric intervention. If there is, however, suggestion that psychiatric intervention might avert suicide such that, when treated, the client would feel differently about ending his life, the question of such an intervention must be debated with the client – if not by the counsellor, then by the GP or mental health professional.

## Common Side Effects of Psychotropic Medication

See Tables 4.5 to 4.8. These lists are not exhaustive and are intended only as a guide. The authors do not accept responsibility for any errors or omissions. A reasonably up to date copy of the *British National Formulary* (BMA/Royal Pharmaceutical Society), known as the BNF, is very useful. New anti-depressants are currently appearing very frequently and information on them should be sought from the BNF.

**Table 4.5** *Side effects of anti-depressants*

*Anti-depressants take at least two to three weeks to achieve therapeutic effect. Often not prescribed in therapeutic dosage for depression by GPs. Need to be taken regularly every day to be effective. Not addictive.*

| Name | Used in | Effects/side effects |
|------|---------|---------------------|
| **Tricyclic anti-depressants** | Depression (>125 mg) Panic disorder Anxiety | Dry mouth, blurred vision, constipation, urinary retention, fits, heart arrythmias, weight gain. Generally dangerous in overdose except Lofepramine |
| e.g. Dothiepin (*Prothiaden*) Imipramine (*Tofranil*) Amitriptyline (*Tryptizol*) Lofepramine (*Gamanil*) Clomipramine (*Anafranil*) | Also obsessional states | Most toxic in overdose<br><br>Safer in overdose and fewer side effects |
| **SSRIs (Selective Serotonin Re-uptake Inhibitors)** | Depression Obsessional states Panic disorder | Nausea and vomiting Agitation and anxiety Weight loss, dizziness, tremor, insomnia, headaches, sweating, Safe in overdose. No weight gain. |
| e.g. Fluvoxamine (*Faverin*) Paroxetine (*Seroxat*) Fluoxetine (*Prozac*) Sertraline (*Lustral*) | Also bulimia nervosa | |
| **MAOIs (Monoamine Oxidase Inhibitors)** There are two types: **Older:** e.g. Phenelzine (*Nardil*) | Depression | Drowsiness, headache, dizziness, stomach upsets, agitation, fits. Many foods and drugs must be avoided (a treatment card is provided with tablets by pharmacist: ignoring this can be dangerous). |
| **Newer:** Moclobemide (*Manerix*) | | Sleep problems, dizziness, nausea, headache, agitation. Foods need not be avoided but over-the-counter drugs such as cold cures must not be taken. |

*continued overleaf*

**Table 4.5**   *Side effects of anti-depressants (contd.)*

| Name | Used in | Effects/side effects |
| --- | --- | --- |
| **Others:** | | |
| Mianserin (*Norval*) | Depression | Less used now, can cause serious anaemia so regular blood tests needed. Not toxic. |
| Trazodone (*Molipaxin*) | Depression | Very sedative. Less toxic. |
| Flupenthixol (*Fluanxol*) | Depression Anxiety | Not really an effective anti-depressant |

**Table 4.6**   *Side effects of major tranquillisers*

*Sedative but not addictive, though can cause serious movement disorders if taken for very long periods. Benefits need to be weighed against side effects.*

| Name | Used in | Side effects |
| --- | --- | --- |
| **Older:** | | |
| e.g. Chlorpromazine (*Largactil*) | High dose psychosis | Movement disorders: Parkinsonism (tremor/rigidity), |
| Thioridazine (*Melleril*) | Low dose anxiety | restless legs, spasms, |
| Trifluperazine (*Stelazine*) | | movements of face and mouth. |
| Haloperidol (*Haldol*) | | Drowsiness, rashes, sun sensitivity, jaundice, fits, menstrual problems, anaemias |
| **Newer:** | | |
| e.g. Sulpiride, pimozide | Schizophrenia | Less than above |
| Injections: | | |
| e.g. Fluphenazine (*Modecate*) | Psychotic illness | As above, long-lasting effect |
| Flupenthixol (*Depixol*) | Usually schizophrenia | |

Proprietary (brand) names in italics.

**Table 4.7** *Side effects of common drugs used in anxiety*

*Useful only when taken for limited periods, and preferably avoided. Addictive. Counselling has been demonstrated to be as beneficial in anxiety disorders, and counselling interventions can be of benefit in withdrawal (see below). Limited course (5–10 days) used in withdrawal from alcohol.*

| Name | Used in | Side effects |
|---|---|---|
| **Minor tranquillisers** | | |
| e.g. Diazepam (*Valium*) Chlordiazepoxide (*Librium*) Nitrazepam (*Mogadon*) Lorazepam (*Ativan*) Temazepam (*Normison*) | Anxiety. Alcohol withdrawal and night sedation | All very addictive, particularly Lorazepam. Forms of temazepam much abused by drug users who inject capsules. Can all cause drowsiness and confusion. |
| **Beta Blockers** | | |

*Used in anxiety. Do not affect psychological symptoms such as worry, tension and fear, but do reduce physical symptoms of anxiety such as palpitations, sweating and tremor. Not addictive.*

| Name | Used in | Side effects |
|---|---|---|
| e.g. Propranolol (*Inderal*) | High blood pressure | lightheadedness, sleep problems, nausea. Not to be used in diabetes or certain types of chest disease. |
| Oxprenolol (*Trasicor*) | Heart disease and lower dose in anxiety | |

Proprietary (brand) names in italics.

**Table 4.8** *Lithium*

*Used to prevent episodes of depression and manic-depressive illness and also in association with anti-depressants in the treatment of depression which has not responded to anti-depressants alone. (N.B. Some people are now prescribed carbamzepine (Tegretol) instead of lithium for the same indications – it has fewer side effects and is also used in epilepsy.)*

| Name | Used in | Side effects |
|---|---|---|
| Lithium carbonate e.g. *Priadel, Camcolit* | As above Blood levels must be checked *regularly.* | At normal levels, tremor, some thirst At excess levels, thirst, vomiting, diarrhoea, tremor, confusion, death. *Thyroid and kidney function must be checked every six months.* |

Proprietary (brand) names in italics.

# 5

# *Ethical and Legal Issues*

This chapter needs to be located in the context of a general understanding of the current state of ethical and legal concerns in the counselling field. It also needs to be understood against the background of medical law and medical ethics as outlined by texts such as those of Kennedy and Grubb (1994), Mason and McCall Smith (1994) and McClean (1995). Particularly recommended in this area are Bond's (1993a) book on ethics and Cohen's (1992) and Jenkins' (1992, 1996) work on the law and counselling. The concern with ethical and legal issues within counselling has grown in recent years, and as a result of this the current pace of change of understanding in these matters is much greater than in the past. Practitioners need to ensure that they are aware of current issues and developments, and ensure that the implications of these are given full weight in their practice.

In the medical and mental health arena many people combine counselling skills with their other areas of work, such as advocacy, and in such situations it is important to think through the possible difficulties. It cannot be automatically assumed that the combination of two independently valid areas of skills will lead to a summation of beneficial effects, as it may well be the case that some of the assumptions that underlie the two activities may be in opposition or that some activities may make others difficult or impossible. For example, assumptions within some counselling perspectives, such as promoting autonomy and using transference, will be undermined by advocate activity or other direct action. A lack of clarity in ethical areas is apparent in these less charted areas of activity.

One of the assumptions in this book has been that counsellors will carry out a fairly formal assessment of clients when they are seen for the first time. However, the reality is that many counsellors do not practise in this way and would experience a conflict between the assumptions that underlie their theoretical orientation and such practice. For these practitioners an assessment may be made over a longer period and using material as it emerges from sessions. It is not for us to dictate counsellors' theoretical perspectives, but counsellors must note the additional risks attached to ways of working that cannot clearly identify medical and psychiatric risks at the beginning of counselling.

## The Counsellor's Duty of Care

The concept of duty of care in relation to counselling is poorly defined compared with that, say, of the medical profession. Part of the reason for that is the lack of litigation and consequent paucity of case law. The counsellor's duty of care can probably best be summarised by saying she is under an obligation to carry our her work with reasonable care and skill. This clearly will extend to medical and psychiatric matters and mean that, in relation to these, the standards of the profession would be applied to the way in which the counsellor handled them. These standards will include guides to ethics and practice, the main texts on the subject, and the views of leading practitioners (see Cohen, 1992). As far as possible counsellors need in their arrangements with clients to clarify the relationship they have with respect to existing medical and psychiatric conditions, and to make clear the respective rights and duties of both the client and the counsellor when these arise during the course of ongoing work (see Kennedy, 1988: 125).

Currently, the way in which this is likely to be understood is in terms of what is widely practised, but there is a tendency to consider the best possible known response as the yardstick in discussions of this area. It is important to note that the counsellor is also responsible for ensuring that his own health is compatible with meeting the required professional standards with clients. In order for negligence to be proved, it would have to be shown that the counsellor owed a duty of care, that the counsellor's conduct did not conform to the appropriate standard of care, and that harm resulted. Where disagreement exists as to how a particular situation involving medical or psychiatric conditions might be handled, the counsellor is less likely to be open to legal action if she acts in a way that would find support amongst a proportion of responsible practitioners. It is important to be aware, though, that departing from accepted practice is very risky, and that using unconventional or untried approaches to a problem may be more difficult to defend if something goes wrong than if problems follow on from a more usual approach.

In relation to the suicide of a client, the same criteria of appropriate standards of care applies. In this case the three factors that are likely to be crucial in determining whether there has been negligence are the following (Daly, 1993):

- whether the client's suicide was foreseeable;
- whether, if the suicide risk was known or should have been inferred by the counsellor, the counsellor took the appropriate precautionary measures;
- whether the counsellor offered help in a reliable and dependable way.

Counsellors need to be aware of the body of knowledge about suicide and parasuicide, and in particular methods of assessing the degree of risk, such as that provided by Eldrid's *Caring for the Suicidal* (1988). Part of the appropriate standard of care for all clients involves respecting their autonomy and right to confidentiality. Striking the balance between the ethical responsibilities of respecting autonomy and confidentiality on the one hand, and protecting clients from self-destruction on the other, is usefully discussed by Bond (1993b). His conclusion is that generally 'the best practice with regard to suicidal clients works in ways which respect the client's autonomy and right to choose until there are substantial grounds for doubting a client's capacity to take responsibility for himself; and there is a serious risk of suicide and there is the possibility of an alternative way of intervening' (1993b: 122).

He argues that careful assessment of the situation not only provides the best basis for making decisions about suicidal clients, but also provides evidence that duty of care has been honoured. Bond (1993a: 78–94) also discusses many areas of ethical concern with suicidal clients, including those that may arise after a client's suicide. Whilst many counsellors have anxieties about this eventuality, with good management of clients who express suicidal feelings, the actuality is rare.

### Negligent Advice

The giving of bad advice opens up the counsellor to action for negligence, as also does the failure to give advice (Cohen, 1992: 15). This means that counsellors who suspect that there may be an organic or psychiatric cause behind something that a client is discussing should discuss with the client the advisability of consulting his GP if this has not already happened. Because of lack of precedent, it is not entirely clear that failure to do so would be actionable but the risk is best avoided. It is likely that those who work in medical settings would be more open to action than those who do not.

### Ethical Dilemmas Arising in Medical Settings

In medical settings, the responsibilities of the counsellor will include not only those arising out of the counselling setting, but also those arising from being part of the practice or unit (Higgs and Dammers, 1992). One important difference between the counsellor and the rest of the team is that a different understanding of confidentiality is likely to apply. Specifically, there may be an assumption that all knowledge and notes are at least potentially available to the team.

Consequently, there may be an expectation that the counsellor will automatically make available to others disclosures that might affect the clinical judgement of colleagues in dealing with the patient. The counsellor will approach disclosure much more from the point of view of what really has to be disclosed for the patient's or other's safety, than whether other members of the team might find it informative. An allied assumption may be that the counsellor needs to know all the available clinical details on a patient, even those that the patient is not aware of themselves. We have already discussed the problem of unwelcome disclosures that can cloud the focus of the counselling from the counsellor's perspective.

The counsellor also needs to ensure that promises made by colleagues about the effects or the efficacy of counselling, in relation to medical or psychiatric conditions, are not exaggerated or misleading. Where this happens it is generally because of lack of knowledge or misunderstandings, and, especially where counselling is a new part of the service, the counsellor must be prepared to invest a considerable amount of time and energy in educating colleagues where they are not familiar with counselling. In all these areas it is important that such differences in perspective and boundaries are clarified before they arise in relation to clients. It is to be hoped that, where counselling is an established part of the service, guidelines will have been carefully worked out and made available to new counsellors. Problems are more likely to arise where a counselling service is being established for the first time in a medical setting.

Counsellors finding themselves involved in developing such services need to be aware of the difficulties and be prepared both to understand the working culture of the existing service and argue the legitimacy of the specific conditions and boundaries that counselling requires if it is going to be ethical and effective. For clarity, and for future reference, it is desirable that protocols are put in writing so that the context within which the counsellor is working in the organisation is clear to everyone.

Those working in medical settings also need to be aware that their vulnerability to action following a complaint may in certain instances be greater than for others. Cohen says that

> Counsellors who suspect an organic cause for their clients' emotional problems should therefore, as a matter of good practice, discuss with the clients the advisability of having a medical examination. Whether a failure to do so would be actionable remains to be seen, and would probably depend on the setting in which the counselling took place. (1992: 16)

Where counsellors become aware of possible negligence or unprofessional behaviour on the part of colleagues in their team there will normally be a responsibility to take action about this. Appropriate advice about action can often be obtained from the counsellor's professional body or insurers.

Counselling in Medical Settings, a division of BAC, has produced a valuable set of guidelines for the employment of counsellors in general practice (Ball, 1993). These offer recommendations about how counsellors should work as part of a primary health-care team, including the importance of team members understanding one another's roles and resources. They advise that the practice and the counsellor work together in developing a protocol for the service. In the area of confidentiality, which we turn to below, the need for some sharing of information is recognised, but the emphasis is put on negotiating this with clients and not merely assuming it.

## Confidentiality

These comments are based on the discussion of confidentiality and record-keeping by Cohen (1992: 19–24). It is important to recognise that consent to disclose is not generally an absolute. Consent may be implied, it may be confined to specific information and it will generally be to a specific third party, or limited number of parties. A dilemma can arise where the counsellor knows that disclosure must take place, such as where the client's life, or that of someone else, is at risk. In such an instance should the counsellor try to persuade the client to give consent? This goes against most counsellors' ideas about respecting their client's autonomy. However, such persuasion may be seen as valuing autonomy more than not making the attempt to obtain permission and just going ahead with disclosure.

Where disclosure is made without consent, it matters to whom the disclosure is made. To put this in an extreme form, disclosure to a client's GP would be seen very differently from disclosure to the press! A defence for disclosure is where the public interest served by disclosure is greater than that served by maintaining confidentiality, but there are not clear guidelines for weighing this balance. In a particular instance, there is no way of knowing in advance how a court might rule on a matter.

One aspect that is clear is that counsellors cannot legally offer absolute confidentiality, neither can the limits to confidentiality be clearly defined. It is also important to note that current practice indicates that damages for emotional distress following on from breach of confidence may be awarded if the client pays the counsellor directly, but not if the counsellor is a volunteer or paid by a third party such as the NHS. Counsellors also need to clarify for themselves the status of their records and notes in their work setting. In particular, they need to be clear who owns these notes and who has, or potentially may have, access to them.

## BAC Code of Ethics and Practice for Counsellors (BAC, 1993)

As mentioned above, part of the standard of care applied to counsellors is the codes of ethics and practice of the profession. We will look at the relevant sections of the BAC Code, both as an example and as the most well-established and respected code in the counselling profession. The relevant clauses of the Code of Ethics and Practice for Counsellors are in parentheses after each point.

■ In relation to medical and psychiatric issues, counsellors must be careful not to step outside their limits of competence. (A4)

Counsellors need to be sure that where they consider themselves competent in relation to medical and psychiatric matters, this is also the position of the significant others who would become involved if something goes wrong. This will relate both to areas of limit to competence that professional bodies (such as the BAC) or insurers would map out, as well as opinions on the individual involved given by, for example, a supervisor or line manager. Employed counsellors certainly need to discuss such issues with their line manager, and those in private practice need to be aware that this may be an arena in which they are more likely to be vulnerable.

■ The counsellor has a responsibility to monitor his levels of competence and to seek others' views through supervision, consultation, etc. (B 2.2.17)

It is not only important to have supervision and consultancy arrangements set up, but also for the nature and frequency of these to be appropriate. The amount of supervision needs to be related to caseload and the question of minimum frequency is important, because this limits how long a situation can 'drift' without there being an opportunity to talk to a supervisor about it. Supervisees also need to monitor how often supervision actually happens, as what on paper may seem to be an adequate frequency can become inadequate when holidays, illness and other interruptions are taken into consideration.

Also supervisees need to ensure that medical and psychiatric concerns in their clients are regularly brought into supervision.

Even over a week a person's physical or psychological state can seriously deteriorate and this is where consultancy arrangements can be valuable, either as an adjunct to discussing the client in supervision, or in preference when specialised advice is needed. A situation where advice relating to serious medical or psychiatric concerns for a client can be obtained the same day would be ideal. Some voluntary organisations recruit medical practitioners onto their management committees specifically for this purpose. Individual practitioners can often set up some arrangement through their network of professional relationships, and this can be usefully established on a reciprocal basis where the other person needs access to advice about counselling matters. For example, one of the authors has informal arrangements with a GP and a psychiatrist whereby he can ask for advice about medical or psychiatric matters and they can ask his advice about patients. In such arrangements it is important that issues of boundary and confidentiality are clear.

■ Counsellors must be careful not to cross the boundary into giving medical or psychiatric advice or treatment. (B 2.2.5/17)

At first glance this may seem to be straightforward, but in reality the boundary can become blurred. What should the counsellor do if a client requests paracetamol for a headache? If someone falls over on the way to a session, should the counsellor administer first aid? It would seem wise for counsellors not to give or recommend to clients anything that might be considered a drug, however innocuous. Similarly, counsellors should refrain from making recommendations or giving advice about ceasing prescribed medication. In relation to first aid, counsellors should not attempt anything beyond their competence with the exception of extreme emergencies, advice about which is given in the appendices. Clearly, all organisations and establishments should have someone responsible for first aid facilities, and preferably also someone with recognised training. Organisations are covered by health and safety legislation as well as any policies operated by the organisations themselves.

■ There is a responsibility to establish what treatment the client
might already be having. (B 2.2.15)

Clients vary in the degree to which they volunteer information,
either because they have reasons to be concerned about
revealing it, or because they do not think it relevant. As a
result, counsellors need to be proactive in asking rather than
assuming that it will emerge.

■ Permission should be obtained from clients before discussing
the client with medical practitioners. (B 2.2.15)

It should be made clear to the client what the purpose of the
discussion is, and that disclosures from the counsellor to the
medical practitioner will be limited to those that are necessary
to the matters in hand. It is generally accepted that in certain
emergencies it may not be possible to obtain permission.

■ The counsellor has a responsibility to monitor his own physical and mental health and to seek help and/or withdraw from
counselling work as appropriate. (B 2.2.18)

This question has been addressed in an earlier chapter, but it
is worth emphasising that counsellors need to be open to the
advice and assessment of others in coming to decisions in this
very difficult area.

■ It is important that a medical practitioner responsible for the
client is not misled as to the kind or degree of help the
counsellor is offering to the client. (B 2.6.2)

It is better if the counsellor conveys information directly if this
is needed, rather than relying on the client to relay accurately
what is being offered. Such communications should be clear
and not rest on any assumptions about what the GP should be
expected to know about the way counsellors in general or
particular organise their work, or the perspective they take.

■ There is a recognition that threats of self-harm or suicide
constitute complex dilemmas in relation to the possibility of

breaking confidentiality, and that some degree of responsible discretion is needed. (B 4.4; B 4.11)

This area has been dealt with above in our discussions of suicidal risk and of confidentiality.

■ Consultation with supervisors and colleagues is important in attempting to resolve areas of conflicts in ethical principles. (B 8.1)

Often the way forward in relation to an ethical dilemma emerges out of discussions with, and advice from, more than one person. Even where ethical decisions involving the medical and psychiatric arena need to be made quickly, it is important to try to talk to at least one other person about the matter before acting as this will often bring an important perspective to the situation. Sometimes problems that at first appear to need immediate action on reflection do not appear so urgent and further time is then available before having to act. It is often helpful to include in your discussions someone who you think might not agree with you as a safeguard against action based on a collusive process.

### Complaints

The whole area of complaints is one that has come much more to the fore in recent years. The trauma caused to counsellors if a complaint is made is such that it can be tempting to try to avoid the issue with clients. However, there is a responsibility on the counsellor to be aware of clients' rights and to provide them with the appropriate information they need to pursue dissatisfactions and to make complaints (Jenkins, 1992: 166). The whole ethos of complaints in medical settings is undergoing rapid change as a result of the Wilson Report (1994). The aim of the changes is to make the system more straightforward and user-friendly. There are two particular recommendations that may affect counsellors (1994: 74). The first is that community NHS staff need particular training in dealing with complaints because they may not have access to advice from more senior managers or specialist staff. Secondly, it is recommended that purchasers specify complaints procedure requirements in contracts with non-NHS providers.

This clearly has implications for counsellors in the voluntary sector and in independent practice.

## The Position of Supervisors

The ethical position of supervisors is quite a difficult one as they have responsibility for their supervisees' clients, not just for supervisees. Whilst the counsellor is clearly responsible for her work with clients, situations may arise where this is not being fulfilled and the supervisee comes to believe that the situation cannot be resolved purely through the supervision. Examples might be serious mental illness or serious physical signs or symptoms. In such cases supervisors may need to take action, but should take careful advice before doing so, either from their supervisors or from other advisers. Discontinuing supervision is not considered adequately to discharge a supervisor's responsibilities and may open up the way to disciplinary action being taken against the supervisor as well as the counsellor. Unfortunately, the clarification of these areas in relation to supervision is even less developed than in counselling, and supervisors must accept that they operate in areas of responsibility that are not currently clearly defined.

## Conclusion

Whereas sound ethical and legal principles can be applied to the medical and psychiatric dilemmas that emerge during counselling, it has to be recognised that much of this has not been tested out in practice. This should not unduly perturb counsellors, however, provided they operate within the best practice of the profession, including good training and ongoing supervision and professional development.

In particular, counsellors should keep detailed contemporary written records in cases where there is potential difficulty or where usual practice is not followed. Where a potential difficulty becomes an actual one, advice from insurers and independent legal advice should be considered.

# Appendix 1

# Suggested Reading

### Chapter 2    Issues in Ongoing Counselling and Supervision

Abel Smith, A., Irving, J. and Brown, P. (1989) 'Counselling in the medical context', in W. Dryden, D. Charles-Edwards and R. Woolfe, *Handbook of Counselling in Britain*. London: Tavistock/Routledge, pp. 122–33.

Counselman, E.F. and Alonso, A. (1993) 'The ill therapist; therapists' reactions to personal illness and its impact on psychotherapy', *American Journal of Psychotherapy*, 47(4): 591–602.

### Chapter 3    Medical Issues

Berkow, R. and Fletcher, A.J. (eds) (1992) *The Merck Manual of Diagosis and Therapy* (16th edn). Rahway, NJ: Merck.

### Chapter 4    Psychiatric Issues

Gelder, M., Gath, D. and Mayou, R. (1989) *Oxford Textbook of Psychiatry* (2nd edn). Oxford: Oxford University Press.

### Chapter 5    Ethical and Legal Issues

BAC, *Code of Ethics and Practice for Counsellors*.

BAC, *Code of Ethics and Practice for the Supervision of Counsellors*.

Bond, T. (1993a) *Standards and Ethics for Counselling in Action*. London: Sage, chap. 6, 'The Suicidal Client' and chap. 7, 'Counsellor Competence'.

Bond, T. (1993b) 'When to protect a client from self-destruction', in W. Dryden (ed.), *Questions and Answers on Counselling in Action*. London: Sage, pp. 118–23.

# Appendix 2

# Glossary

Most of the specialist medical and psychiatric terms used in this book are defined and explained in the text. Those not so defined are included below, together with others added for convenience of reference.

*Biofeedback* The use of an electrical instrument measuring a physiological variable, such as heart rate or blood pressure, to control certain physical responses. Apart from its use in teaching relaxation, it has also been used with insomnia, epilepsy and *heart arrhythmias*.

*Biophysical* Relating to a physical understanding of a biological problem.

*Bipolar affective disorder* A disorder of mood in which there are episodes of both mania and depression. It is also known as manic-depressive illness.

*Borderline personality* A type of personality disorder difficult to describe precisely and concisely. Such people are impulsive, poor at personal relationships, unpredictable and sometimes can seem to be on the point of losing touch with reality.

*Chemotherapy* The treatment of illness by medication, commonly used particularly in such treatment of cancer.

*Dementia* An organic disorder of the brain involving loss of intellectual ability and memory and also changes of personality. It can be caused by a number of conditions, the most common of which is Alzheimer's disease.

*Electro-convulsive therapy (ECT)* The treatment of mental disorders, particularly depression, by passing an electric current through the brain with the use of anaesthesia and a muscle relaxant.

*Flashbacks* Sudden memories of earlier experiences. There can be a number of causes for this, including a history of traumatic experiences or of taking hallucinogenic drugs.

*Heart arrhythmias* Variations from the normal heartbeat.

*Mania* A state of extreme euphoria and overactivity often involving socially unacceptable behaviour.

*Manic-depressive illness* See *Bipolar affective disorder*.

*Motivational interviewing* An approach to interviewing which aims to help a person to decide whether or not they wish to change their behaviour.

*Neuro-psychological* Relating to the interaction between the brain, and thoughts and behaviour.

*Osteoporosis* A bone disease, especially found in women over 50, involving loss of bone tissue.

*Ovulation* The movement of a human egg towards a woman's uterus, taking place approximately half-way through the menstrual cycle.

*Parasuicide* Deliberate self-harm where suicide is not the actual, and usually not the intended, outcome.

*Parkinson's disease* A progressive disease of the nervous system, usually occurring in later life, and involving tremor and progressive disability.

*Parkinsonism* Symptoms similar to Parkinson's disease but following on from viral infections and some drugs.

*Post-traumatic stress disorder* A disorder caused by a traumatic event outside the range of usual experience, characterised by a cluster of symptoms including anxiety, *flashbacks*, nightmares and guilt.

*Pre-term delivery* A delivery of a baby that occurs before the completion of the full term of pregnancy (37 weeks).

*Psychosocial* Involving both the mind and social factors.

*Schizophrenia* A group of disorders leading to mental deterioration such as distortion of thinking, delusions and a disturbed sense of self.

*Somatic* Relating to the body.

*Somatisation* The expression of psychological problems through physical symptoms.

*Stress inoculation* Working through the 'worst case scenario' in advance of facing the problem as a means of attempting to defuse the potential difficulties and stresses to be faced.

*Systematic desensitisation* A behavioural treatment combining progressive exposure to a feared object or situation together with a method of controlling the person's anxiety arousal.

*Thyroid* A gland near the larynx which produces hormones vital in maintaining normal growth and body functioning.

# Appendix 3

# Counselling in Specific Medical and Psychological Conditions

Clients may request help for medical conditions either to complement physical treatments they are already receiving or instead of such treatment, where they have a firm belief that the problem has a psychological basis, they do not believe in using drug treatments or there is clear evidence that psychological factors do play a part in the genesis of the condition and/or evidence that psychological treatments can be effective.

The following tables are intended as a simple guide to what has been demonstrated to be effective in a range of medical disorders. Specific psychological disorders are also included in this list where there is a defined form of psychological treatment recommended. It is not intended to be an exhaustive list. Particular areas where there is a large and readily available literature (such as HIV counselling or bereavement) have not been included, nor have specialised psychological interventions for schizophrenia which would generally not be carried out by a counsellor. In the following tables an asterisk * indicates that this is primarily a research paper. Other references are more practically based.

| Some specific disorders: medical | Therapeutic model | References |
|---|---|---|
| **Cancer:** | | |
| *Aims of treatment:* | | |
| *General* | Supportive group therapy and self-hypnosis | Moorey and Greer (1989) Spiegel et al. (1989)* Hill et al. (1992)* |
| 1 Reducing anxiety and depression | | |
| 2 Improving mental adjustment | | |
| 3 Promotion of a sense of control and active participation in treatment | | |
| 4 Acquisition of coping strategies | | |
| 5 Improved communication with partner | | |
| 6 Encouragement of open expression of feelings of anger | | |
| *Coping with diagnosis:* | Crisis intervention counselling | Capone et al. (1980)* |
| *Nausea and vomiting with chemotherapy:* | Behavioural interventions: hypnosis, relaxation, systematic desensitization, biofeedback, stress inoculation | Pratt et al. (1984)* |

*continued overleaf*

| Some specific disorders: medical | Therapeutic model | References |
| --- | --- | --- |
| **Pain:** | | |
| Headache | Behavioural interventions: | Blanchard (1979)* |
| Migraine and tension headaches | biofeedback, relaxation training | |
| | Cognitive-behavioural therapy | Perris and Herlofson (1993)* |
| Low back pain | Relaxation training; Cognitive-behavioural therapy | Turner (1982)* |
| Pelvic pain | Cognitive-behavioural therapy | Pearce and Erskine (1989) |
| Consider also possible co-existence of depression, marital conflict, eating disorder or history of sexual abuse | Relaxation | |
| **Hypertension:** (high blood pressure) | Behavioural interventions: biofeedback, relaxation training: effects variable and may *not* be long-term | Jacob et al. (1987)* |
| **Diabetes mellitis:** | | |
| *Aims of treatment:* | | |
| *Coping with complications in young people* | 'Group counselling': aimed at discussing difficulties and 'meaning' behind the symptoms | Shillitoe (1988) |

| | | |
|---|---|---|
| *Poor blood glucose control in young people* | Family therapy | Minuchin et al. (1978) |
| **Multiple sclerosis:**<br>*Coping with the implications of the diagnosis and its complications* | Non-directive counselling | Segal (1991)<br>ARMS: Action for Research into MS, 4a Chapel Hill, Stansted, Essex CM24 8AG provides back-up service for counsellors |
| **Infertility:** | Non-directive counselling | Shaw (1991)<br>Jennings (1995)<br>British Infertility Counselling Association, Dept of Obstetrics and Gynaecology, Hammersmith Hospital, Du Cane Road, London W12 |

| Some specific disorders: psychological | Therapeutic model | References |
| --- | --- | --- |
| **Depression:** | Cognitive-behavioural therapy | Perris and Herlofson (1993)* |
|  | Interpersonal therapy | Elkin et al. (1989)* |
|  | Psychodynamic psychotherapy | Shapiro et al. (1995)* |
| **Anxiety:** |  |  |
| *Generalised anxiety* | Cognitive and/or behavioural | Perris and Herlofson (1993)* |
| *Panic disorder* | therapies | Cottraux (1993)* |
| *social phobia* |  |  |
| *Agoraphobia* |  |  |
| *Obsessive compulsive disorder* | Behaviour therapy |  |
| **Marital problems:** | Behaviour therapy | Gurman et al. (1986)* |
|  |  | Langsley et al. (1993)* |
|  | Integrated model | Will and Wrate (1985) |

**Eating disorders:**
*Bulimia nervosa*

| | |
|---|---|
| Cognitive-behavioural therapy | Cox and Merkel (1989)* |
| | Freeman et al. (1988)* |
| Behaviour therapy | Fairburn et al. (1991)* |
| Family therapy: various models | Langsley et al. (1993)* |

**Excessive alcohol/drugs:**

| | |
|---|---|
| Analytic or cognitive-behavioural | Mason (1995) |
| | Woody et al. (1986)* |
| Motivational interviewing | Chick et al. (1985)* |
| | Miller and Rollnick (1991) |
| Controlled drinking | Emmelkamp (1986)* |

# Appendix 4

## Useful Organisations

British Association for Counselling
1 Regent Place, Rugby, Warwickshire CV21 2PJ

British Association for Sexual & Marital Therapy
PO Box 62, Sheffield S10 3TL

Counselling in Primary Care Trust
First Floor, Majestic House, High Street, Staines TW18 4DG

UK Council for Psychotherapy
167–169 Great Portland Street
London W1N 5NB; tel. 0171-436 3002

# Appendix 5

# Internet Addresses

There is a rapidly increasing amount of information available on the Internet. Because it is rapidly changing, some of the following addresses may not work. However, pages often include links to other sites and you should anyway be able easily to build up your own list. Current useful sites include:

*Internex Online Mental Health Information*
http://www.io.org/~madmagic/help/help/html#search

*Mind Homepage*
http://www.shef.ac.uk/~is/mind/home.hmtl

*Mind Links to World Wide Web Resources*
http://www.shef.ac.uk/~is/mind/links.hmtl

*Pharmaceutical Information*
http://pharminfo.com/

*Psychiatry Online*
http://www.cityscape.co.uk/users/ad88/psych.htm

# Appendix 6

# Preparation for Termination of Practice

This is the procedure suggested by the British Association for Sexual and Marital Therapy to its counsellors and psychotherapists for winding up a practice and the appointment of an executor in the event that the counsellor is too ill to do so or dies suddenly, and is used with their kind permission.

## Introduction

Therapists have a duty and a responsibility to make arrangements so that clients with whom they are working are informed as soon as possible in the event of their own incapacity due to illness, change of circumstances or death. They also have a duty to ensure that the confidentiality of their clients' records will be maintained. Clients can be informed of these arrangements if they wish, and indeed it may be of therapeutic relevance in dealing with issues of separation, mortality and death.

In NHS or agency practice, management should also consider the application of the following principles detailed below.

1   It is recommended that therapists make a will, including the appointment of a therapeutic executor. The will should give instructions regarding the filing system and ongoing referral of clients, trainees and supervisees, if relevant, and the disposal of professional books, lecture notes and other material. The

will should make it clear that all executors have a duty to maintain confidentiality regarding clients and clients' records.

2   The therapeutic executor should be reimbursed for time involved and expense incurred and, in the event of the therapist's death, will need to be in contact with the estate executors.

3   A list of colleagues should be included in the instructions to the therapeutic executor, since it is usually unrealistic to expect one colleague to be able to deal with a whole caseload. Colleagues may be needed to help with bereavement and transitional work, to cover groups, supervision and training and, where requested, to continue therapy.

4   The therapeutic executor should contact ongoing clients as soon as possible, informing them of the situation and offering support from another therapist to deal with immediate issues, if possible. If clients wish, their records could be passed to the next therapist.

5   The therapeutic executor will contact the therapist's accountant and send all relevant documents so that the financial aspects of the practice can be settled. Where there is no accountant, these documents may be passed to the estate executors.

6   Proper attention must be given to the disposal of client records in whatever form, taking into account the protection of clients, context of practice ownership of records and therapists' wishes.

The ongoing care and welfare of clients is the primary consideration at all times in the work of the therapeutic executor.

# Appendix 7

---

# The Mental Health Act (1983)

This Act applies only to England and Wales. Scotland and Northern Ireland have their own similar legislation. The sections of the Act which are most likely to be met in practice are:

1  Emergency and short-term orders for assessment for up to 28 days (Sections 2 and 4). These apply to any mental disorder, which does not need to be specified.
2  Longer term orders for treatment (Section 3). These apply only to four specified types of disorder:

*Mental Illness*: is not defined but the Act states that a person should not be treated as suffering from mental disorder 'by reason only of promiscuity, or other immoral conduct, sexual deviancy or dependence on alcohol or drugs'.

*Severe Mental Impairment*: associated with abnormally aggressive or seriously irresponsible conduct.

*Mental Impairment*: similar to above but of lesser degree.

*Psychopathic Disorder*: with associated aggressive conduct.

An *Approved Social Worker* (ASW) is one approved by the local authority as having special experience of mental illness.

An *Approved Doctor* is one who has been approved under Section 12 of the Act as having special experience of mental disorder and is usually a psychiatrist.

*Section 4: Admission for assessment in case of emergency*
Much less commonly used now (as potentially much more open to abuse of persons' rights). Lasts 72 hours. Application must be made by ASW (most usually) or nearest relative (rarely), either of whom must have seen the patient in the last 24 hours. Requires only one doctor who is usually, in practice, the GP. Used only where waiting for a second doctor would cause undesirable delay.

*Section 2: Admission for assessment*
Lasts up to 28 days. Application by ASW or nearest relative. Requires two doctors, one of whom must be approved and the other who should preferably know the patient (usually GP). Used to detain someone who is either a risk to themselves or to other people and needs admission to hospital. The patient has the right to appeal.

*Section 3: Admission for treatment*
Lasts up to six months in the first instance. Application by ASW or nearest relative as before. Requires two doctors, as for Section 2. Nature of disorder is specified. Used to detain someone who is either a risk to themselves or to other people and needs admission to hospital for treatment to be carried out. The patient has the right to appeal.

*For further information see the appendix of* The Oxford Textbook of Psychiatry *(2nd edition) (Gelder, Gath and Mayou, 1989) published by Oxford University Press: a useful standard text of psychiatry.*

# Appendix 8:

# A Classification of Personality Disorder

The classification presented here is an amalgamation of that found in ICD-10 and DSM-IV. Personality disorder can be defined as *'deeply ingrained, inflexible maladaptive patterns of relating to, perceiving and thinking about the environment and oneself which are of sufficient severity to cause either significant impairment in adaptive functioning or subjective distress'*. This is generally recognisable about the time of adolescence. Many people show traits of a range of abnormalities.

| | |
|---|---|
| *Paranoid* | Sensitive, suspicious and may be jealous. Often litigious. |
| *Affective* | Lifelong abnormality of mood which may be depressive, elated, changing from one to the other (cyclothymic). |
| *Schizoid* | Withdrawn, introspective and detached. Indifference to social relationships. Restricted range of emotional experience and expression. |
| *Explosive* | Uncontrollable outbursts of aggression, physical or verbal but not otherwise antisocial. |
| *Obsessive/compulsive* | Rigid, compulsive, inflexible and perfectionist. |
| *Histrionic* | Sometimes called 'hysterical'. Demanding and attention-seeking, emotionally shallow. (Often an abusive label applied |

|  | without due grounds to 'difficult' female patients by male doctors.) |
|---|---|
| *Dependent* | Inability to cope with normal demands. Submissive. |
| *Antisocial* | Commonly called 'psychopaths' or 'sociopaths'. Antisocial behaviour with absence of conscience, inability to learn from mistakes, a long history of disturbance and often violence and problems with the law. Often described as superficially very charming and 'plausible'. |
| *Narcissistic* | Grandiose, self-important, hypersensitive to the evaluation of others. |
| *Borderline* | Instability of mood, interpersonal relationships and self-image. Short-lived psychotic episodes. |
| *Passive-aggressive* | Passive resistance to demands for adequate social and occupational performance. Sulky, resentful, avoids obligations. |
| *Multiple personality* | Not strictly a personality disorder but a dissociative or hysterical disorder which is a type of neurotic illness. Existence within the person of two or more distinct personalities or personality states which recurrently take full control of the person's behaviour. (Be wary of creating more 'personalities' simply by demonstrating interest in their possible existence!) |

# Appendix 9

# Dealing with Medical Emergencies

Very occasionally, a client will become acutely ill during a counselling session. Although such illness may represent a manifestation of the client's psychological difficulties, it may equally represent a biophysical disease process. It is better to err on the side of safety and to assume biophysical disease if there is any doubt. Whether or not the client suffers permanent physical harm may well depend upon the counsellor's actions. This section will deal with the immediate care of a limited number of acute clinical problems. Further information about these and other problems is contained in the excellent *First Aid Manual* (Marsden et al., 1992).

## Unconsciousness

Unconsciousness is defined as a state in which a person cannot be roused by non-painful stimuli. There are many causes, but the immediate management is that of the state of unconsciousness, not of the cause. The steps to be taken are in the following order:

- Check that the client's air passages are not obstructed and that he or she is breathing adequately. It may be necessary to turn the client's head to one side and use a finger to hook dentures or other obstruction from the mouth or throat. In order to find out whether the client is breathing, look, listen and feel for signs of respiration.

- Check that the client has a pulse. Use your index and middle finger to feel for the carotid pulse just below the angle of the jaw, in the hollow between the voice box and adjoining muscle. (If you are not sure of the location, it is easy to feel in your own neck.)
- Place the client in the recovery position as shown in Figure 1. (This is not appropriate in the case of suspected spinal injury.)
- Cover the client with a coat or blanket.
- Stay with the client to ensure that respiration continues unimpeded, and send for an ambulance or immediate medical help.

**Exhaled-air Ventilation**

If an unconscious client has a pulse but does not breathe despite removal of any obstruction from the airway, then exhaled air ventilation should be started:

- Roll the client onto his or her back.
- Tilt the head back, pinch the nose in order to block the nostrils and open the client's mouth with a hand on the point of the jaw.
- Take a deep breath in, seal your lips round the client's mouth and blow into the lungs. As you do so, watch the chest to check that it rises. Take about two seconds for a full inflation. If the chest fails to rise, the airway is not fully open or there is a blockage which you have failed to find. Tilt the head back further and try again. If the chest still fails to rise then check again for a blockage.
- Remove your mouth from that of the client and watch the chest fall. Take a deep breath and repeat the inflation.
- After ten inflations, check the pulse. If the heart is still beating then continue exhaled-air ventilation at a rate of ten inflations per minute. Check the pulse after every ten inflations.
- If you have not yet had the opportunity to call for help, do so after the first ten inflations.
- If the client starts to breathe independently, then place him or her in the recovery position.
- If the heart stops beating, then start external cardiac compression (see below).

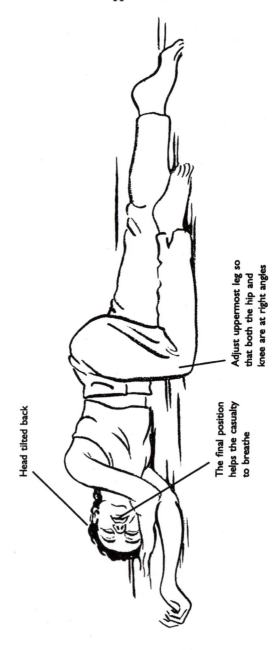

Head tilted back

The final position helps the casualty to breathe

Adjust uppermost leg so that both the hip and knee are at right angles

**Figure 1** *The recovery position*

A number of devices have been developed that remove the need for direct physical contact between the mouth of an unconscious person and the mouth of a person giving exhaled-air ventilation. These are available through surgical suppliers and some pharmacists.

### External Cardiac Compression

The heart of somebody who stops breathing may continue to beat for several minutes. If exhaled-air ventilation is started during that time then the heart may carry on beating and maintain an adequate circulation of blood to the brain and throughout the person's body. Conversely, if a person's heart stops beating, then he or she will stop breathing within a matter of seconds. A patient whose heart has stopped beating will need external cardiac compression in addition to exhaled-air ventilation. If you cannot feel a pulse in a patient in whom you are giving or about to start giving exhaled-air ventilation, then:

- Telephone for an ambulance if you have not done so already.
- Roll the client onto his or her back and give two breaths of exhaled-air ventilation, as described above.
- Kneel alongside the client beside his or her chest. Place the heel of one hand along the line of the breast-bone (sternum) in its lower third. Cover this hand with the heel of your other hand and interlock your fingers.
- Kneel over the client so that your shoulders are directly over the breast-bone and your arms straight. Keeping your arms straight, press down vertically to move the breast-bone 4–5 cms. Release the pressure. Compressions should be regular and smooth, not jerky or jabbing, and given at a rate of 80 per minute.
- Complete 15 compressions. Then move to beside the client's head and give two more breaths of exhaled-air ventilation. Continue with a cycle of 15 compressions followed by two ventilations.
- If you have assistance, then one person continues with chest compressions at a rate of 80 per minute, while the other gives exhaled-air ventilation at a rate of one inflation every five

compressions. Stop the compressions to ensure that the client's chest rises during inflation, but do not wait for it to fall before restarting.

■ Do not interrupt what you are doing to check the pulse unless you think that the heart may have started beating again. If the pulse does return then stop external cardiac compression but continue with exhaled-air ventilation, checking the pulse after every ten inflations, until independent breathing returns. Then place the client in the recovery position and continue to monitor the pulse and breathing.

Training in basic resuscitation techniques including exhaled-air ventilation and external cardiac compression is widely available and highly recommended.

### Fits

Fits may be a manifestation of epilepsy, drug use, alcohol withdrawal, previous head injury or other, less common causes. Although fits may occasionally reflect psychological processes rather than biophysical disease, the immediate management is the same whatever the cause.

People with epilepsy are sometimes aware that they are going to have a fit. A fit typically starts with the person losing consciousness and falling to the ground, perhaps with a cry. He or she then becomes rigid for a few seconds and may stop breathing during this time. Rhythmic jerking movements start, becoming increasingly vigorous and often accompanied by noisy breathing. After a variable interval, the jerking becomes less powerful until the person is left relaxed and unconscious. Again the period of unconsciousness is extremely variable and may be followed by an interval in which the person appears to have recovered but acts bizarrely or inappropriately. During a fit the most important thing to do is to save the client from injury. This may occur as a result of the initial fall, or during the phase of jerking. You should make no attempt to put anything into the mouth. If the client remains unconscious after the convulsion has finished, then subsequent management is that of unconsciousness, as described above. Once consciousness has been regained then the client should not be left alone until it is clear that he or she is well orientated and behaving appropriately. There is no need to send for an ambulance unless the client has several fits or is injured, or unless the fit lasts more than 15 minutes from onset until recovery. If you do not call an ambulance, you should assist your client in obtaining medical advice the same day.

## Acute Chest Pain and Acute Shortness of Breath

Any new pain in the chest or shortness of breath may be an indication of serious heart or lung disease. The client should be helped to sit or lie comfortably. He or she may carry tablets or other medication to take for the symptoms, in which case the client should be encouraged to do so.

You should phone for urgent medical advice, either from the client's general practitioner or another doctor. If such advice is not readily available, or if the client appears distressed or ill in any way, then send for an ambulance.

## Physical Harm and Poisoning

Clients may injure or poison themselves either intentionally or otherwise. First aid for physical injury depends on the site, cause and type of injury; the *First Aid Manual* (Marsden et al., 1992) gives clear and authoritative advice in this situation. You should not take any action that puts yourself or others at risk. Unless the injury is clearly trivial then medical advice should be sought, or the client should be referred to a local Accident and Emergency department. If the injury is self-inflicted then you should also consider arranging urgent psychiatric assessment.

Poisons may be swallowed, inhaled, absorbed through the skin or (rarely) injected. The commonest mode of intentional self-poisoning is by mouth, often using drugs that have been pre-scribed or otherwise acquired. You should make no attempt to induce vomiting in a client who has swallowed drugs or other poisons. In the case of an inhaled poison you should remove the client from the source of harm, provided that it is safe to do so, and into fresh air. Poisons on the skin should be flushed away with plenty of cold water. Even if the client appears entirely well, medical advice should always be sought following definite or possible poisoning. If the client appears ill in any way, then call an ambulance.

Management of the unconscious, poisoned client is as described above in the section on unconsciousness. If the client stops breathing, then take extreme care that you do not expose yourself to an inhaled or corrosive poison during exhaled-air ventilation.

# References

*ABPI Data Sheet Compendium* (1994–95, revised annually). London: Datapharm Publications.

American Psychiatric Association (1994) *Desk Reference to the Diagnostic Criteria from DSM-IV*. Washington, DC: American Psychiatric Press.

BAC (1993) *Code of Ethics and Practice for Counsellors*. Rugby: British Association for Counselling.

Ball, V. (1993) *Guidelines for the Employment of Counsellors in General Practice*. Rugby: Counselling in Medical Settings/BAC.

Bennett, G. (1990) *Treating Drug Abusers*. London: Routledge.

Berke, J.H. (1979) *I Haven't Had to Go Mad Here: The Psychotic's Journey from Dependence to Autonomy*. London: Pelican.

Berkow, R. and Fletcher, A.J. (1992) *The Merck Manual of Diagnosis and Therapy*. Rahway, NJ: Merck.

Blake, F., Gath, D. and Salkovskis, P. (1995) 'Psychological aspects of premenstrual syndrome: developing a cognitive approach', in R. Mayou, C. Bass and M. Sharpe (eds), *Treatment of Functional Somatic Symptoms*. Oxford: Oxford University Press.

Blanchard, E.B. (1979) 'Behavioural treatment for headaches', *Progress in Behaviour Modification*, 8: 207–47.

Bond, T. (1993a) *Standards and Ethics for Counselling in Action*. London: Sage.

Bond, T. (1993b) 'When to protect a client from self-destruction', in W. Dryden (ed.), *Questions and Answers on Counselling in Action*. London: Sage, pp. 118–23.

British Medical Association/Royal Pharmaceutical Society (1995) *British National Formulary* (revised annually). London.

Broome, A.K. (ed.) (1989) *Health Psychology*. London: Chapman & Hall.

Capone, M.A., Good, R.S., Westie, S. and Jacobsen, A.F. (1980) 'Psychosocial rehabilitation in gynaecologic oncology patients', *Archives of Physical Medicine & Rehabilitation*, 61: 128–32.

Chick, J., Lloyd, G. and Crombie, E. (1985) 'Counselling problem drinkers in medical wards: a controlled study', *British Medical Journal*, 290: 965–7.

Clare, A. (1988) *Psychiatry in Dissent: Controversial Issues in Thought and Practice*, 2nd edn. London: Routledge.

Clinical Standards Advisory Group (1994) *Back Pain*. London: Her Majesty's Stationery Office.

Cohen, K. (1992) 'Some legal issues in counselling and psychotherapy', *British Journal of Guidance and Counselling*, 20: 10–26.

Cooper, C.W. (1993) 'Vestibular neuronitis: a review of a common cause of vertigo in general practice', *British Journal of General Practice*, 43: 164–7.

Cooper, I.S. (1973) *The Victim is Always the Same*. New York: Harper & Row.

Cope, H., David, A., Pelosi, A. and Mann, A. (1994) 'Predictors of chronic post viral fatigue', *Lancet*, 344: 864–8.

Cottraux, J. (1993) 'Behaviour therapy', in N. Sartorius, G. De Girolamo, G.A. Andrews German and L. Eisenberg (eds), *Treatment of Mental Disorders: A Review of Effectiveness*. Washington, DC: World Health Association and American Psychiatric Press.

Counselman, E.F. and Alonso, A. (1993) 'The ill therapist; therapists' reactions to personal illness and its impact on psychotherapy', *American Journal of Psychotherapy*, 47(4): 591–602.

Cox, G.L. and Merkel, W.T. (1989) 'A qualitative review of psychosocial treatments for bulimia', *Journal of Nervous and Mental Diseases*, 177: 77–84.

Crisp, A. (1990) *Anorexia Nervosa*. New York: W.B. Saunders Company.

Daly, R.J. (1993) 'Suicide in depressed patients', *British Journal of Psychiatry*, 163 (suppl. 20): 29–32.

Davidson, R., Rollnick, S. and MacEwan, I. (1991) *Counselling Problem Drinkers*. London: Routledge.

Davis, H. and Fallowfield, L. (1991) *Counselling and Communication in Health Care*. Chichester: Wiley.

Dickson, A. and Henriques, N. (1992) *Menopause: The Woman's View*. London: Quartet Books.

Doll, H., Brown, S., Thurston, A. and Vessey, Y.M. (1989) 'Pyridoxine (vitamin B6) and the premenstrual syndrome: a randomised cross-over trial', *Journal of the Royal College of General Practitioners*, 39: 364–8.

Eldrid, J. (1988) *Caring for the Suicidal*. London: Constable.

Elkin, I., Shea, T. and Watkins, J. (1989) 'National Institute of Mental Health treatment of depression collaborative research program: general effectiveness of treatments', *Archives of General Psychiatry*, 46: 971–82.

Emmelkamp, P. (1986) 'Behaviour therapy with adults', in S.R. Garfield and A.E. Bergin (eds), *Handbook of Psychotherapy and Behavior Change*, 3rd edn. New York: John Wiley.

Eysenck, H. (1992) 'The outcome problem in psychotherapy', in W. Dryden and C. Feltham (eds), *Psychotherapy and its Discontents*. Buckingham: Open University Press, pp. 100–34.

Eysenck, H.J. and Grossarth-Maticek, R. (1991) 'Creative novation behaviour therapy as a prophylactic treatment for cancer and coronary heart disease: Part II, Effects of treatment', *Behaviour Research and Therapy*, 29: 17–31.

Fairburn, C.G. and Hope, R.A. (1988) 'Disorders of eating and weight', in R.E. Kendell and A.K. Zealley (eds), *Companion to Psychiatric Studies*. Edinburgh: Churchill Livingstone.

Fairburn, C., Jones, R., Peveler, R. et al. (1991) 'Three psychological treatments in bulimia nervosa: a comparative trial', *Archives of General Psychiatry*, 48: 463–9.

Farthing, M.J.G. (1995) 'Irritable bowel, irritable body or irritable brain?', *British Medical Journal*, 310: 171–5.

Fernando, S. (1988) *Race and Culture in Psychiatry*. London: Croom Helm.

France, R. and Robson, M. (1986) *Behaviour Therapy in Primary Care: A Practical Guide*. London: Chapman and Hall.

Frank, R.T. (1931) 'The hormonal causes of premenstrual tension', *Archives of Neurology and Psychiatry*, 26: 1053–7.

Freeman, C.P.L., Barry, F., Dunkeld Turnbull et al. (1988) 'Controlled trial of psychotherapy for bulimia nervosa', *British Medical Journal*, 296: 521–5.

Freud, S. (1962) 'The question of lay-analysis', in *Two Short Accounts of Psycho-Analysis*. Harmondsworth: Penguin.

Friedman, G. (1991) 'Treatment of the irritable bowel syndrome', *Gastroenterology Clinics of North America*, 20: 325–33.

Gardner, W.N. and Bass, C. (1989) 'Hyperventilation in clinical practice', *British Journal of Hospital Medicine*, 41: 73–81.

Gask, L. (1995) 'Management in primary care', in R. Mayou, C. Bass and M. Sharpe (eds), *Treatment of Functional Somatic Symptoms*. Oxford: Oxford University Press.

Goldberg, L., Gask, L. and O'Dowd, T. (1989) 'The treatment of somatisation: teaching the techniques of reattribution', *Journal of Psychosomatic Research*, 33: 689–95.

Greer, G. (1991) *The Change*. London: Hamish Hamilton.

Grol, R. (ed.) (1981) *To Heal or to Harm: The Prevention of Somatic Fixation in General Practice*. London: Royal College of General Practitioners.

Grossarth-Maticek, M. and Eysenck, H.J. (1991) 'Creative novation behaviour therapy as a prophylactic treatment for cancer and coronary heart disease: Part I – description of treatment', *Behaviour Research and Therapy*, 29: 1–16.

Gurman, A., Kniskern, D. and Pinsof, W. (1986) 'Research on the process and outcome of marital and family therapy', in S.R. Garfield and A.E. Bergin (eds), *Handbook of Psychotherapy and Behavior Change* (3rd edn). New York: John Wiley.

Guthrie, E., Creed, F.M. and Dawson, D. (1993) 'Controlled study of psychotherapy in irritable bowel syndrome', *British Journal of Psychiatry*, 163: 315–21.

Hammersley, D. (1995) *Counselling People on Prescribed Drugs*. London: Sage.

Hawton, K. (1985) *Sex Therapy: A Practical Guide*. Oxford: Oxford University Press.

Haynes, R.B., Sackett, D.L., Taylor, D.W., Gibson, E.S. and Johnson, A.L. (1978) 'Increased absenteeism from work after detection and labelling of hypertensive patients', *New England Journal of Medicine*, 299: 741–4.

Higgs, R. and Dammers, J. (1992) 'Ethical issues in counselling and primary care', *British Journal of Guidance and Counselling*, 20(1): 27–38.

Hill, D.R., Kelleher, D. and Shumaker, S.A. (1992) 'Psychosocial interventions in adult patients with coronary heart disease and cancer: a literature review', *General Hospital Psychiatry*, 14: 28S–42S.

Holmes, G.P., Kaplan, J.E., Gantz, N.M., Komaroff, A.L., Schonberger, L.B., Straus,

S.E., Jones, J.F., Dubois, R.E., Cunningham-Rundles, C., Pahwa, S., Tosato, G., Zegans, L.S., Purtilo, D.T., Brown, N., Schooley, R.T. and Brus, I. (1988) 'Chronic fatigue syndrome: a working case definition', *Annals of Internal Medicine*, 108: 387–9.

Ho-Yen Do (1990) 'Patient management of post-viral fatigue syndrome', *British Journal of General Practice*, 40: 37–9.

Humphrey, M. (1989) *Back Pain*. London: Tavistock/Routledge.

Hunter, M. (1994) *Counselling in Obstetrics and Gynaecology*. Leicester: BPS Books.

Jacob, R.G., Wing, R. and Shapiro, A.P. (1987) 'The behavioural treatment of hypertension: long-term effects', *Behaviour Therapy*, 18: 325–52.

James, W. (1960) *The Varieties of Religious Experience*. Glasgow: William Collins.

Jayson, M.I.V. (1994) 'Mechanisms underlying chronic back pain', *British Medical Journal*, 309: 681–2.

Jenkins, P. (1992) 'Counselling and the law', *Counselling* (Aug.): 165–7.

Jenkins, P. (1997) *Counselling, Psychotherapy and the Law*. London: Sage.

Jennings, S. (1995) 'Fertility', in J. Keighley and G. Marsh (eds), *Counselling in Primary Health Care*. Oxford: Oxford University Press.

Kaplan, H.S. (1987) *The Illustrated Manual of Sex Therapy*. New York: Brunner Mazel.

Kelleher, D. (1988) *Diabetes*. London: Tavistock/Routledge.

Kendell, R.E. (1975) *The Role of Diagnosis in Psychiatry*. Oxford: Blackwell.

Kennedy, I. (1988) *Treat Me Right: Essays in Medical Law and Ethics*. Oxford: Clarendon Press.

Kennedy, I. and Grubb, A. (1994) *Medical Law*. London: Butterworth.

Kettell, J., Jones, R. and Lydeard, S. (1992) 'Reasons for consultation in irritable bowel syndrome: symptoms and patient characteristics', *British Journal of General Practice*, 42: 459–61.

Kramer, P. (1994) *Listening to Prozac*. London: Fourth Estate.

Lacey, J.H. (1983) 'Bulimia nervosa, binge eating and psychogenic vomiting: a controlled treatment study and long-term outcome', *British Medical Journal*, 286: 1609–13.

Laing, R.D. and Esterson, A. (1970) *Sanity, Madness and the Family*. Harmondsworth: Penguin.

Lambert, M.J., Shapiro, D.A. and Bergin, A.E. (1986) 'The effectiveness of psychotherapy', in S.R. Garfield and A.E. Bergin (eds), *Handbook of Psychotherapy and Behavior Change* (3rd edn). New York: John Wiley.

Langsley, D.G., Hodes, M. and Grimson, W.R. (1993) 'Psychosocial interventions', in N. Sartorius, G. De Girolamo, G.A. Andrews German and L. Eisenberg (eds), *Treatment of Mental Disorders: A Review of Effectiveness*. Washington, DC: World Health Association and American Psychiatric Press.

Lawrie, S.M. and Pelosi, A.J. (1994) 'Chronic fatigue syndrome: prevalence and outcome', *British Medical Journal*, 308: 732–3.

Lazarus, A.A. (1989) *The Practice of Multimodal Therapy*. Baltimore: Johns Hopkins University Press.

Levy, S.M. (1990) 'Humanizing death: psychotherapy with terminally ill patients', in G.M. Herek et al. (eds), *Psychological Aspects of Serious Illness: Chronic*

*Conditions, Fatal Diseases and Clinical Care.* Washington, DC: American Psychological Association, pp. 185–213.

McCarty, T., Schneider-Braus, K. and Goodwin, J. (1986) 'Use of alternate therapist during pregnancy leave', *Journal of the American Academy of Psychoanalysis*, 14(3): 377–83.

McClean, S. (1995) *Medical Law.* Aldershot: Dartmouth.

McLeod, S. (1981) *The Art of Starvation: An Adolescence Observed.* London: Virago.

Marsden, A.K., Moffatt, C. and Scott, R. (1992) *First Aid Manual. The Authorised Manual of St. John Ambulance, St. Andrew's Ambulance Association, and the British Red Cross* (revised regularly). London: Dorling Kindersley.

Maslow, A.H. (1943) 'A theory of human motivation', *Psychological Review*, 50: 370–96.

Mason, J.K. and McCall Smith, R.A. (1994) *Law and Medical Ethics.* London: Butterworth.

Mason, P. (1995) 'Substance misuse', in J. Keithley and G. Marsh (eds), *Counselling in Primary Health Care.* Oxford: Oxford University Press.

Mental Health Foundation (1990) *Mental Illness: The Fundamental Facts.* London: Mental Health Foundation.

Mental Health Foundation (1992) *Guidelines for the Prevention and Treatment of Benzodiazepine Dependence.* London: Mental Health Foundation.

Miller, W.R. and Rollnick, S. (1991) *Motivational Interviewing: Preparing People to Change Addictive Behaviour.* New York: Guildford Press.

Minuchin, S., Rosman, B.L. and Baker, L. (1978) *Psychosomatic Families: Anorexia Nervosa in Context.* Cambridge, MA: Harvard University Press.

Moorey, S. and Greer, S. (1989) 'Adjuvant Psychological Therapy: a cognitive behavioural treatment for patients with cancer', *Behavioural Psychotherapy*, 17: 177–90.

Mynors-Wallis, L. (1995) 'Randomised controlled trial comparing problem-solving treatment with amitriptyline and placebo for major depression in primary care', *British Medical Journal*, 310: 441–6.

Nicolson, P. (1992) 'The construction of female psychology', in J.T.E. Richardson (ed.), *Cognition and the Menstrual Cycle.* New York: Springer-Verlag.

Orbach, S. (1978) *Fat is a Feminist Issue.* London: Hamlyn.

Palmer, S. and Dryden, W. (1995) *Counselling for Stress Problems.* London: Sage.

Passmore, H.S. (1973) 'The patient's use of his doctor', in E. Balint and J.S. Norell (eds), *Six Minutes for the Patient.* London: Tavistock.

Paykel, E. and Priest, R. (1992) 'Guidelines for the detection and management of depression: a consensus statement', *British Medical Journal*, 305: 198–202.

Pearce, S. and Erskine, A. (1989) 'Chronic pain', in S. Pearce and J. Wardle (eds), *The Practice of Behavioural Medicine.* Oxford University Press: British Psychological Society.

Pearce, S. and Wardle, J. (eds) (1989) *The Practice of Behavioural Medicine.* Oxford: BPS Books.

Pearson, R. (1990) *Asthma Management in Primary Care.* Oxford: Radcliffe Medical Press.

Pelosi, A.J. and Appleby, L. (1992) 'Psychological influences on cancer and ischaemic heart disease', *British Medical Journal*, 304: 1295–8.

Pendleton, D., Schofield, T., Tate, P. and Havelock, P. (1984) *The Consultation: An Approach to Learning and Teaching*. Oxford: Oxford University Press.

Perris, C. and Herlofson, J. (1993) in N. Sartorius, G. De Girolamo, G.A. Andrews German and L. Eisenberg (eds), *Treatment of Mental Disorders: A Review of Effectiveness*. Washington, DC: World Health Association and American Psychiatric Press.

Persaud, R. (1993) 'Talk your way out of trouble', *Sunday Times*, 26 September.

Pfeffer, J.M. and Waldron, G. (1987) *Psychiatric Differential Diagnosis*. Edinburgh: Churchill Livingstone.

Pollin, I.P. (1995) *Medical Crisis Counselling*. New York: Norton.

Pratt, A., Lazar, R.M., Penman, D. and Holland, J.C. (1984) 'Psychological parameters of chemotherapy induced conditioned nausea and vomiting: a review', *Cancer Nursing* (December): 483–9.

Quinn, N. (1995) 'Parkinsonism – recognition and differential diagnosis', *British Medical Journal*, 310: 447–52.

Rack, P. (1982) *Race, Culture and Mental Disorder*. London: Tavistock.

Richards, J.P. (1990) 'Postnatal depression: a review of recent literature', *British Journal of General Practice*, 40: 472–6.

Richardson, J.T.E. (1989) 'Student learning and the menstrual cycle: premenstrual symptoms and approaches to studying', *Educational Psychology*, 9: 215–38.

Ridsdale, L., Evans, A. and Jerrett, W. (1993) 'Patients with fatigue in general practice: a prospective study', *British Medical Journal*, 307: 103–6.

Robinson, I. (1988) *Multiple Sclerosis*. London: Tavistock/Routledge.

Royal College of Psychiatrists (1987) *Drug Scenes: A Report on Drugs and Drug Dependence*. London: Royal College of Psychiatrists.

Ryle, A. and Beard, H. (1993) 'The integrative effect of reformulation: cognitive analytic therapy with a patient with borderline personality disorder', *British Journal of Medical Psychology*, 66: 249–58.

Sacks, O. (1986) *The Man who Mistook his Wife for a Hat*. London: Pan.

Scambler, G. (1989) *Epilepsy*. London: Tavistock/Routledge.

Scott, M.J. and Stradling, S.G. (1992) *Counselling for Post-Traumatic Stress Disorder*. London: Sage.

Segal, J. (1991) 'Counselling people with multiple sclerosis and their families', in H. Davis and L. Fallowfield (eds), *Counselling and Communication in Health Care*. Chichester: Wiley.

Shapiro, D., Barkham, M., Rees, A. et al. (1995) 'Decisions, decisions, decisions: determining the effects of treatment method and duration on the outcome of psychotherapy for depression', in M. Aveline and D. Shapiro (eds), *Research Foundations for Psychotherapy Practice*. Chichester: John Wiley/Mental Health Foundation.

Sharpe, M., Hawton, K., Simkin, S., Surawy, C., Hackmann, A., Klimes, I., Peto, T., Warrell, D. and Seagroatt, V. (1996) 'Cognitive behaviour therapy for the chronic fatigue syndrome: a randomised controlled trial', *British Medical Journal*, 312: 22–6.

Shaw, P. (1991) 'Infertility counselling', in H. Davis and L. Fallowfield (eds), *Counselling and Communication in Health Care*. Chichester: Wiley.

Shillitoe, R.W. (1988) *Psychology and Diabetes: Psychological Factors in Management and Control*. London: Chapman & Hall.

Sibbald, B., Addington-Hall, J., Brenneman, D. et al. (1993) 'Counsellors in English and Welsh general practices: their nature and distribution', *British Medical Journal*, 306: 29–33.

Sibbald, B., White, P., Pharoah, C., Freeling, P. and Anderson, H.R. (1988) 'Relationship between psychological factors and asthma morbidity', *Family Practice*, 5: 12–17.

Spiegel, D., Bloom, J.R., Kraemer, H.C. and Gottheil, E. (1989) 'Effect of psychosocial treatment on survival of patients with metastatic breast cancer', *Lancet* (October): 888–91.

Striano, J. (1988) *Can Psychotherapists Hurt You?* Santa Barbara, CA: Professional Press, pp. 5–31.

Styron, W. (1992) *Darkness Visible*. London: Picador.

Sutherland, S. (1987) *Breakdown: A Personal Crisis and a Medical Dilemma*. Oxford: Oxford University Press.

Taylor, S.E. and Aspinwall, L.G. (1990) 'Psychosocial aspects of chronic illness', in G.M. Herek et al. (eds), *Psychological Aspects of Serious Illness: Chronic Conditions, Fatal Diseases and Clinical Care*. Washington, DC: American Psychological Association, pp. 3–60.

Tuckett, D., Boulton, M., Olson, C. and Williams, A. (1985) *Meetings Between Experts*. London: Tavistock.

Turner, J.A. (1982) 'Comparison of group progressive relaxation training and cognitive-behavioural group therapy for chronic low back pain', *Journal of Consulting & Clinical Psychology*, 50: 757–65.

Usherwood, T. (1987) 'Factors affecting estimates of the prevalence of asthma and wheezing in childhood', *Family Practice*, 4: 318–21.

Usherwood, T.P. (1990) 'Responses to illness – implications for the clinician', *Journal of the Royal Society of Medicine*, 83: 205–7.

Ussher, J.M. (1992) 'The demise of dissent and the rise of cognition in menstrual-cycle research', in J.T.E. Richardson (ed.), *Cognition and the Menstrual Cycle*. New York: Springer-Verlag.

Waddell, G. (1993) 'Simple low back pain: rest or active exercise?', *Annals of Rheumatic Disease*, 52: 317–19.

Walker, M. (1990) *Women in Therapy and Counselling*. Milton Keynes: Open University Press.

Walton, J.N. (1989) *Essentials of Neurology*. London: Pitman.

Wessely, S., Chalder, T., Hirsch, S. et al. (1995) 'Postinfectious fatigue: prospective cohort in primary care', *Lancet*, 345: 1333–8.

WHO (1993) *The ICD-10 Classification of Mental and Behavioural Diseases*. Geneva: WHO.

Will, D. and Wrate, R.M. (1985) *Integrated Family Therapy: A Problem-Centred Psychodynamic Approach*. London: Tavistock.

Wilson Report (1994) *Being Heard: The Report of the Review Committee on NHS Complaints Procedures*. London: HMSO.

Woody, G.E., McLellan, A.T., Lubursky, L. et al. (1986) 'Psychotherapy for substance abuse', *Psychiatric Clinics of North America*, 9: 547–62.

Worden, W.J. (1991) *Grief Counselling and Grief Therapy: A Handbook for the Mental Health Practitioner* (2nd edn). London: Routledge.

# Index

abnormal movements, 42–4, 74–5
*ABPI Data Sheet Compendium*, 39–40
acquired immune deficiency syndrome
    (AIDS), 55, 57
advocacy, 99, 107
agoraphobia, 90, 126 Appendix
AIDS *see* acquired immune deficiency
    syndrome
AIDS dementia, 57
akinesia, 43
Alcoholics Anonymous, 79–80
alcohol problems, 42, 79–80, 83, 127
    Appendix
Alonso, A., 26
*American Psychiatric Association*
    *Diagnostic and Statistical Manual*
    *(DSM-IV)*, 73
angina, 45–6
anorexia nervosa, 75–6
anorgasmia, 78
anti-depressants, 90, 93–5
    side effects, 103, 104–5 Table 4.5
anti-hypertensive drugs, 53
anxiety, 77, 89–92 & Table 4.3, 126
    Appendix
    and dyspnoea, 44–5
    and insomnia, 77
    and palpitations, 47
    side effects of drugs used in, 106
        Table 4.7
    and tranquilliser withdrawal, 102
    and tremor, 42
appearance and mental health
    problems, 73–5

appetite gain/loss, 75–6
Approved Social Workers (ASWs), 70,
    132 Appendix
assessment, 10–17, 18, 19, 108
assessment questionnaires, 19
asthma, 44
athetosis, 43

'baby blues', 61
*BAC Code of Ethics and Practice for*
    *Counsellors*, 113–16
back pain, 50–2, 124 Appendix
Beck Depression Inventory, 94
behavioural nurse specialists, 70
benign essential tremor, 42
Bennett, G., 81
Berkow, R., 58
binge eating, 76
biological model, 68
biophysical processes, 37–8, 65
blood pressure, high, 52–3, 124
    Appendix
Bond, T., 29, 107, 109
borderline personality disorder, 99, 100,
    135 Appendix
brain imaging, 68
breath, shortness of, 44–5, 141
    Appendix
*British National Formulary*, 39–40, 103
Broome, A. K., 13
bulimia nervosa, 76, 127 Appendix

cancer, 46, 49, 123 Appendix
carbamazepine, 96

care plans, 6–7
case conferences, 7
chest pain, 45–6, 141 Appendix
childbirth *see* pregnancy and childbirth
chlorpromazine, 96, 105 Table 4.6
chorea, 43
chronic fatigue syndrome, 49–50
chronic illness/disability, 13, 53–4
    in counsellors, 30
chronic pain, 54
climacteric, 62–3
clinical psychologists, 70, 91–2, 101
'co-categorisation', 56–7
cognitive analytic therapy (CAT), 99
cognitive-behavioural therapy (CBT),
    76, 78, 94, 101
Cohen, K., 107, 111, 112
Community Mental Health Teams
    (CMHTs), 69, 70, 71
community psychiatric nurses (CPNs),
    70
'compensation neurosis', 39, 51
complaints, 116–17
compulsions, 87–8
confidentiality, 21–2, 57, 83, 109, 110,
    112
confusion, 97
consultancy arrangements, 114
Cooper, I. S., 12
coprolalia, 44
counselling sessions, gaps in, 23–5
counsellors
    illness in, 26–31, 115
    pregnancy in, 31–4
    visible disability/disfigurement in,
        31
Counselman, E. F., 26
creative novation therapy, 46
Crisp, A., 75
cultural context and mental illness, 67

Davidson, R. et al., 79
'debriefing', 91
delirium, 97
delusional mood, 86
delusional perceptions, 86
delusions, 85–7, 94, 101

delusions of reference, 86
dementia, 57, 65–6, 75, 97
denial, 12, 25, 30
depression, 50, 65, 92–5 & Table 4.4,
    126 Appendix
    and anxiety, 90
    and back pain, 52
    counselling contra-indicated, 101–2
    and cultural context, 67
    and delusions, 86, 87, 94
    and deterioration of self-care, 74
    and fatigue, 49
    and hallucinations, 89, 94
    and headache, 40
    and insomnia, 77
    major, 92–5
    and menopause, 63
    and obsessional thoughts, 88
    and overeating, 76
    post-natal, 61, 71, 79
    and premenstrual syndrome, 78
    prevalence in community, 68–9
    and psychomotor retardation, 75, 83,
        84, 93
    secondary, 92
    and sexual problems, 77
    and speech, 83, 84
    and suicide, 103
    and violent behaviour, 83
dermatitis artefacta, 73
diabetes mellitus, 124 Appendix
diagnoses, psychiatric, 66, 73
diet and health, 57–9
disease concept, 65
disorientation, 97
dizzy spells, 47
drug problems, 80–1, 82 Table 4.1, 127
    Appendix
*Drug Scenes*, 80
drug side effects, 39–40, 43, 53, 103,
    104–6 Tables 4.5–4.8
Dryden, W., 13
duty of care, 108–10
dying clients, 20, 21, 24–6
dysmorphophobia, 74
dyspareunia, 78
dyspepsia, 47–8

dyspnoea, 44–5, 141 Appendix
dystonia, 43

eating disorders, 75–6, 127 Appendix
ECT (electro-convulsive therapy), 75, 95
Eldrid, J., 109
emergencies, 46, 76, 97, 114, 136–42 Appendix
ethical issues, 3–5, 21–2, 29–30, 107–17
excitement, 95–7
exhaled-air ventilation, 137–9 Appendix
exophthalmos, 42
external cardiac compression, 139–40 Appendix
Eysenck, H. J., 46

factitious symptoms, 39, 51
family therapy, 76
fatigue, 49–50
Fernando, S., 67
first aid, 114, 136–42 Appendix
*First Aid Manual*, 136 Appendix, 141 Appendix
fits, 140–1 Appendix
Fletcher, A. J., 58
'flight of ideas', 84
food additives, 58–9
forgetfulness, 97–8

gastrointestinal symptoms, 47–9
generalised anxiety disorder, 42, 90, 126 Appendix
general practitioners, 8–10, 21, 22, 71, 98–9
goitre, 42
Goldberg, L. et al., 98
grief, 93
Grubb, A., 107

hallucinations, 89, 94, 101
haloperidol, 96, 105 Table 4.6
Hammersley, D., 102
Hawton, K., 77
headache, 37–8, 40–2, 124 Appendix

health beliefs, 38–9
Health Visitors, 71
heart disease, 44, 45–6, 47
hidden issues, 18–20
HIV *see* human immunodeficiency virus
HIV seroconversion illness, 55
hormone replacement therapy, 62, 63
hospitalisation of clients, 23–4
hot flushes, 62
human immunodeficiency virus (HIV), 54–7
hypertension, 52–3, 124 Appendix
hyperthyroidism, 42
hypochondriasis, 86, 90, 98
hypomania, 83–4, 95–6

*ICD-10 Classification of Mental and Behavioural Diseases*, 73
ideas of reference, 86
illness behaviour, 39
illness in counsellors, 26–31, 115
illusions, 89
impotence, 77–8
infectious illness in counsellors, 29
infertility, 125 Appendix
insomnia, 77
interpersonal therapy (IPT), 94
irritable bowel syndrome, 48–9

Jenkins, P., 107

Kaplan, H. S., 77
Kennedy, I., 107
Korsakoff syndrome, 58

legal issues, 107–17
    *see also* Mental Health Act (1983)
Levy, S. M., 25
limits of competence, 29–30, 113
lithium, 42, 95, 96, 106 Table 4.8
low back pain, 51, 124 Appendix
lung disease, 44–5, 46

McCall Smith, R. A., 107
McClean, S., 107
McLeod, S., 75

major tranquillisers, 43, 96, 105 Table 4.6
mania
  and appearance, 74
  and delusions, 86, 87
  and hallucinations, 89
  and insomnia, 77
  and overexcitement, 95–7
  and speech, 84
  and violent behaviour, 83
  and weight loss, 75
manic-depressive illness, 96–7, 101, 102
marital problems, 126 Appendix
Maslow, A. H., 57–8
Mason, J. K., 107
medical advice/treatment by counsellors, 114
medical conditions, 37–64
  assessment of undiagnosed, 12–13
  counselling in specific conditions, 122–5 Appendix
medical emergencies, 46, 76, 97, 114, 136–42 Appendix
medical settings, dilemmas in, 8–10, 20–2, 110–12
memory impairment, 12, 97–8
menopause, 62–3
Mental Health Act (1983), 67–8, 132–3 Appendix
Mental Health Foundation, 102
mental health problems, serious, 66, 73–106
mental health professionals, 69–73
mental illness
  prevalence in community, 68–9
  use of term, 65–8, 132 Appendix
migraine, 38, 40–1, 124 Appendix
minor tranquillisers
  side effects of, 106 Table 4.7
  withdrawal from, 102
mixed affective state, 96
moclobemide, 94–5, 104 Table 4.5
models in psychiatry, 68
monoamine oxidase inhibitors (MAOIs), 94–5 104 Table 4.5
mood changes, 89–97

morbid jealousy, 83
movement disorders, 42–4, 74–5
multiple sclerosis, 125 Appendix
myalgic encephalomyelitis, 49–50
myoclonus, 43

neck pain, 51
negligent advice, 110
night sweats, 62
non-medical settings, dilemmas in, 22–3

obsessions and compulsions, 87–8, 126 Appendix
occupational therapists, 71
organic brain disease, 87, 89, 97
osteoporosis, 63
overeating, 76
over-inclusiveness, 84
over-valued ideas, 86

pain, 124 Appendix
  back, 50–2, 124 Appendix
  chronic, 54
  and sexual problems, 62, 78
Palmer, S., 13
palpitations, 47
panic disorder, 45, 90, 91–2, 126 Appendix
Parkinsonism, 43
Parkinson's disease, 42–3
Paykel, E., 94
Pearce, S., 13
perimenopause, 62–3
personality disorders, 66, 81, 99, 100
  classification, 134–5 Appendix
Pfeffer, J. M., 73
phobias, 90, 91–2
physical illness *see* medical conditions
physical symptoms and psychiatric illness, 98–9
physical trauma and headache, 41
poisoning, 141–2 Appendix
Pollin, I. P., 13
post-menopausal bleeding, 62
post-natal depression, 61, 71, 79

post-traumatic stress disorder (PTSD), 91

post-viral fatigue syndrome, 49–50

poverty of speech, 84

practice nurses, 71

pregnancy and childbirth, 31–4, 60–2, 79

premature ejaculation, 78

premenstrual syndrome (PMS), 59–60, 78–9

prescribed drugs, side effects of, 39–40, 43, 53, 103, 104–6 Tables 4.5–4.8

'pressure of speech', 83–4

Priest, R., 94

problem-solving therapy, 94

professionals and conflicts of view, 13–16

Prozac, 95

psychiatric advice/treatment by counsellors, 114

psychiatric conditions, 65–106
    assessment of undiagnosed, 10–12
    counselling in specific conditions, 122 Appendix, 126–7 Appendix
    in counsellors, 30
    exacerbated by counselling, 15–16, 99–102

psychiatric hospitalisation, 23–4

psychiatrists, 66–7, 69

psychiatry, 65
    models in, 68

psychodynamic counselling, 29, 30

psychogenic vomiting, 76

psychomotor retardation, 75, 83, 84, 93

psychosocial processes, 37–8

psychotherapists, 69–70

psychotropic drugs, side effects of, 43, 103, 104–6 Tables 4.5–4.8

pyridoxine (vitamin B6), 59

Rack, P., 67

referrals, 1–10, 16–17, 20

referrer's agenda, 2–3

referring on, 16

regression, 100

rituals, 87–8

Sacks, O., 44

schizoaffective disorder, 96–7

schizophrenia, 65, 68–9
    counselling contra-indicated, 101
    and cultural context, 67
    and delusions, 86, 87, 101
    and dysmorphophobia, 74
    and hallucinations, 89, 101
    and mania, 96–7
    Schneider's First Rank Symptoms, 85 & Table 4.2
    and speech, 84
    and thought disorder, 84–5
    and violent behaviour, 83
    and weight loss, 75

'schizophrenogenic family', 101

Schneider's First Rank Symptoms, 85 & Table 4.2

sciatica, 51

Scott, M. J., 91

scurvy, 58

secondary gain, 39, 51

selective serotonin re-uptake inhibitors (SSRIs), 94, 95, 104 Table 4.5

self-care, deterioration of, 74

self-harm, 73, 74, 115–16, 141–2 Appendix

self-mutilation, 73, 74

self-referrals, 3–5

serious mental health problems, 66, 73–106

sexual problems, 77–8

signs, 37

sleep problems, 77

social workers (SWs), 70

somatisation, 98

speech, oddness of, 83–4

standard referral forms, 2

Stradling, S. G., 91

strange experiences, 89

strange ideas, 84–8

Striano, J., 12

stupor, 74–5

Styron, W., 102
substantia nigra, 43
sudden delusional ideas, 86
suicidal behaviour, 56, 95, 102–3,
    109–10, 115–16
supervisors, 16–17, 25–6, 34–5,
    113–14, 117
Sutherland, S., 102
symptoms, 37
syndrome concept, 65

tension headache, 40, 124 Appendix
terminal illness
    in clients, 20, 21, 24–6
    in counsellors, 29–31
termination of practice, 29–31, 130–1
    Appendix
termination of pregnancy, 60–1
therapeutic executors, 130–1
    Appendix
thought broadcasting, 85
thought disorder, 84–5, 97
thought insertion, 85
thought withdrawal, 85
thyrotoxicosis, 42
tics, 43–4
torticollis, acute, 51

Tourette's syndrome, 43–4
tranquillisers *see* major *and* minor
    tranquillisers
tremor, 42–3, 74
tricyclic anti-depressants, 94, 95, 104
    Table 4.5

unconsciousness, 136–7 Appendix
unconscious processes, 39
United Kingdom Council for
    Psychotherapy, 69–70
Ussher, J. M., 59

vaginismus, 78
vertigo, 47
violent behaviour, 81–3
visible disabilities/disfigurements in
    counsellors, 31
vitamins, 58, 59

Waldron, G., 73
Wardle, J., 13
weight gain/loss, 75–6
wills, making by counsellors, 30–1,
    130–1 Appendix
Wilson Report (1994), 116
Worden, W. J., 93